HOW TO FYAIL IN DIGITAL TRANSFORMATION

7 MOST IMPACTFUL TOPICS EXPLORED

Limiting Beliefs | Resolving Conflicts | Achieving Organizational Alignment | Leveraging Resistance | Measuring what Matters | Mastering Accountability | Maximizing Value Delivered

Alina Aronova, Asmita Malse Dharap, Jennifer Clarke-Burke, Jennifer Greve, Naomi Kent, Nadia Clifford, Natalie Vinitsky, Tatiana Thomas

LUBA SAKHARUK

When we FYAIL, we grow!

Let's get excited to FYAIL!

Let's FYAIL together!

First published by Ultimate World Publishing 2022
Copyright © 2022 Luba Sakharuk

ISBN

Paperback - 978-1-922714-48-0
Ebook - 978-1-922714-49-7

Luba Sakharuk has asserted her rights under the Copyright, Designs and Patents Act 1988 to be identified as the author of this work. The information in this book is based on the author's experiences and opinions. The publisher specifically disclaims responsibility for any adverse consequences which may result from use of the information contained herein. Permission to use information has been sought by the author. Any breaches will be rectified in further editions of the book.

All rights reserved. No part of this publication may be reproduced, stored in or introduced into a retrieval system, or transmitted in any form, or by any means (electronic, mechanical, photocopying, recording or otherwise) without the prior written permission of the author. Any person who does any unauthorized act in relation to this publication may be liable to criminal prosecution and civil claims for damages. Enquiries should be made through the publisher.

Cover design: Ultimate World Publishing
Layout and typesetting: Ultimate World Publishing
Editor: Maddie Johnson

Ultimate World Publishing
Diamond Creek,
Victoria Australia 3089
www.writeabook.com.au

Disclaimer

Ninety-nine percent of the stories shared in this book are based on reality. Names and some details have been modified to respect privacy.

Dedication

To my daughters: You are my pride, purpose, and most meaningful WHY in life!

Although this book does not solely focus on "Women in **STEM** (Science, technology, engineering, and mathematics)" or "Women in Technology" per se, it is a story about a woman who found herself in the male-dominated corporate world, navigating through challenging interactions, learning what matters most and becoming a solid leader herself. Through various examples from one woman's career, you will gain insight into the corporate world and understand the importance of **Facing Yet Another Important Lesson** in any challenge that may come your way!

When we **replace the fear of failing with the excitement of learning**, we first and foremost **reduce unnecessary stress** and have an extremely high chance **to succeed** in digital transformations and so much more in life!

To all readers who expressed interest in this book: Thank you for your curiosity!

To Become a Contributor...

Email your bio along with a short blurb on why you would like to collaborate to luba@lubasakharuk.com with a **Subject Line: Contributing to future book(s)**

The next opportunity to collaborate is on the following book,

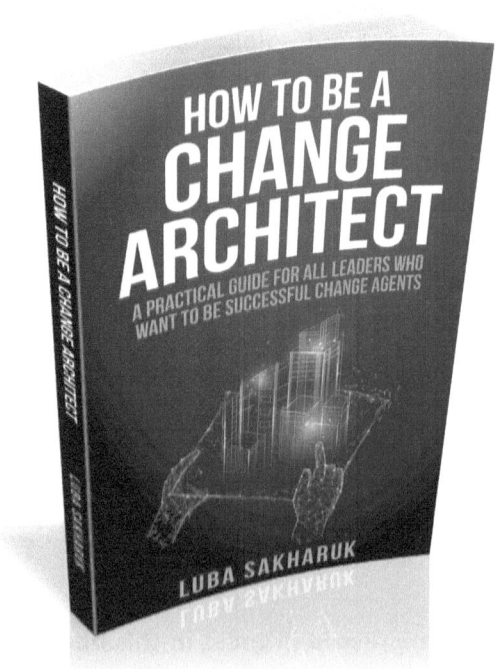

Other Books by Luba Sakharuk

Testimonials

"I worked with and gleaned valuable and insightful information from Luba's mastery as a facilitator. Her skills, talent and innate ability to listen, understand and engage individuals and groups and then facilitate meaningful and productive discussions can only be described as "part of her chemical makeup." Whether speaking to individuals on a personal or professional level, addressing groups or executives, Luba's knack for articulating an assembly's process into a simplistic and succinct form entices change for an otherwise reluctant audience. Her ability to clearly listen, ingest, comprehend and restate a speaker's intent is admirable and demonstrates discerning observation expertise. Luba's positive outlook is obvious in her conversations and demeanor and is only matched by her radiating and contagious energy. What may appear as subtle character traits are intentional expressions of authenticity, patience and intellect."

Connie Betts PSM, PMP, BRMP, SSBB
Senior Manager
Engineering Enablement

"Organizational change is challenging. Luba is comfortable having difficult conversations to understand what people believe their barriers to success are. She personalizes her coaching approach to each person to help them build confidence and succeed. Her passion is helping people develop a growth mindset. Luba embraces learning and loves to share her knowledge via engaging workshops and inspiring keynote delivery. Luba's positive approach to life is contagious."

Linda Wells, Agile Coach

"It is World's Woman Day, March 8th, and it is my honor to write a testimonial for this amazing book by Luba Sakharuk, where she invites us to join Vita's journey as a woman in tech.

The digital world we are living in made it possible for Luba and I to meet and build a connection between Boston and Zurich. I am an agile mindset expert. This means I support people and teams in their thinking, feeling, and acting agile, which is also referred to as BEING agile. It is necessary in order for agile transformation to really happen. Embracing frameworks alone isn't enough.

When Luba asked me to write the testimonial for her book, I felt blessed and honored. Our goals and values align where my mission too is to support other people in any transformation and to increase their conscious awareness for personal development.

The book you are holding in your hands now lets you tune in in a woman's journey in tech and lets you experience her own transformation. You get the perspective of a person who is part of a transformation as well of the perspective of someone supporting others by guiding, mentoring, leading and inspiring them to embrace their own journeys. This book's format makes it a very easy read. Through the stories shared, which read like a novel, you will learn the journey of the main character going from a developer to a successful consultant who shares her experience along the way, extracting and sharing different lessons with the reader.

I love her attitude and the message that FYAIL is just yet another learning opportunity. She has a great and empathic way to guide people on their journey. It is incredible how openly and selflessly she shares her valuable knowledge in this book and beyond. This book provides various exercises at the end of each chapter as well, which encourages you to reflect and make whatever journey you are currently on your own experience. This book is brilliant and I highly recommend it. Follow the exercises, take a deeper dive with every question asked and do not allow anyone to stop you! It will support you in your personal transformation, as well the agile and/or digital transformation your company may be going through as well. Read it, enjoy it, and have fun."

Zurich March 8 2022
Stephanie Schuster, Agile mindset expert
www.stephyschuster.com

Contents

Disclaimer	vii
Dedication	ix
To Become a Contributor…	x
Other Books by Luba Sakharuk	xi
Testimonials	xii
Introduction	1
What is Digital Transformation?	5
What is Agile Transformation?	7
What are Limiting Beliefs?	9

Chapter 1: Limiting Beliefs — 11
- About the Stories in this Chapter 15
- 1.1 Becoming a Digital Transformation Coach 19
- 1.2 Getting Comfortable Being Uncomfortable 23
- 1.3 Becoming a Manager 27
- 1.4 Getting a Mentor 29
- 1.5 Becoming a Consultant 32
- 1.6 Becoming an Independent Consultant/Business Owner 35
- 1.7 Getting Over the Fear of Being a Salesperson 38
- 1.8 Business Owner vs. Entrepreneur 39
- 1.9 Becoming a Board Member 43
- 1.10 Limiting Beliefs in Digital Transformations 47
- 1.11 Exercise 48

Chapter 2: Resolving Conflict — 51
- About the Stories in this Chapter 55
- 2.1 When There Are Conflicting Priorities 57
- 2.2 Disagreeing with a Client 62

2.3 Preventing Conflict 66
2.4 Disagreeing with Higher-Ups 72
2.5 Having Different Perspective.. 76
2.6 Acting as a Servant Leader: "How Can I Help?" 80
2.7 Questioning Your Own Emotional Intelligence................... 84
2.8 Understanding Communication
    Styles for Effective Collaboration.. 88
2.9 Common Causes for a Conflict in Digital Transformation.... 92
2.10 Exercise 94

Chapter 3: Achieving Organizational Alignment — 97
About the Stories in this Chapter 101
3.1 Defining Organizational Change 105
3.2 North Star, Vision, and Outcomes vs Outputs 107
3.3 Applying Change Management 110
3.4 Setting a Vision 114
3.5 Setting Priorities 119
3.6 Organizational Alignment in the Context of
    a Digital Transformation.. 123
3.7 Exercise 124

Chapter 4: Leveraging Resistance — 127
About the Stories in this Chapter 131
4.1 Defining the "Thing that Doesn't Work" 135
4.2 Converting from Kicking to Cheering 138
4.3 Building Relationships and Trust 140
4.4 Being Creative in Breaking the Ice..................................... 147
4.5 Meeting People Where They Are 151
4.6 Having Empathy Towards People 153
4.7 Change Fatigue 156
4.8 Exercise... 158

Chapter 5: Measuring What Matters — 161
About the Stories in this Chapter 165
5.1 Why Measure?.. 169
5.2 How Do You Know What Matters? 171
5.3 Velocity 172

Contents

    5.4 KPIs vs OKRs 175
    5.5 Having a Baseline Across the Organization 178
    5.6 Measuring Quality 180
    5.7 Measuring Behavior 188
    5.8 Measuring Success of a Digital Transformation 192
    5.9 Exercise 196

Chapter 6: Mastering Accountability   **199**
    About the Stories in this Chapter 203
    6.1 Basic Expectations of Behavior 207
    6.2 Solving the Right Problem 211
    6.3 Who is Accountable for Culture? 214
    6.3.1 Exercise 217
    6.3.2 Exercise 218
    6.4 Who is Accountable for a Successful
        Digital Transformation? 220
    6.5 Exercise 222

Chapter 7: Maximizing Value Delivered   **225**
    About the Stories in this Chapter 229
    7.1 What is Value? 233
    7.2 Value Definition Workshop 236
    7.3 Maximizing Value as a Product Owner 239
    7.4 Maximizing Value as a Coach 251
    7.5 Maximizing Value as a Leader 253
    7.6 Maximizing Internal Value with Automation 256
    7.7 Maximizing Value as a Change Agent 261
    7.8 Maximizing Value of a Digital Transformation 263
    7.9 Exercise 266

Conclusion   **269**
About Author   **273**
About Contributing Authors   **275**
Acknowledgements   **289**
Call to Action   **291**
Glossary   **293**

Introduction

"It's a journey, and the sad thing is you only learn from experience, so as much as someone can tell you things, you have to go out there and make your own mistakes in order to learn."
— EMMA WATSON

Emma Watson is best known for playing the character of Hermione Granger, one of Harry Potter's best friends in the Harry Potter books and movies. In the Harry Potter series, Hogwarts is a boarding school of witchcraft and wizardry. In this unbelievably fantastic school of magic, students have conflicts, face challenges, and endure many learning opportunities. There are not-so-nice people with agendas and leaders who protect and risk their own lives. There are miscommunications, blame, a ton of stressful moments and at the same time, there is teamwork and extraordinary camaraderie.

We could draw parallels between limiting beliefs, challenges we face, and lessons we learn in the corporate world with those in this engaging storyline of wizards and magic. There are so many scary and stressful moments in the Harry Potter books and movies that one might wonder, *how in the world did Harry Potter face it all? Where did Hermione find the courage?* I doubt they were looking at everything they faced as a learning opportunity, nor were they excited to replace fear with it. But we, in the corporate world, thankfully aren't fielding hexes and curses, although it may feel this way sometimes! We can and should be encouraged to replace our fears with the excitement of learning!

This book is written for anyone whose day-to-day is in the corporate high-tech world, going through innovation, agile, and/or digital transformation and adapting to new ways of working.

As transformational leaders, our job is to listen, understand, describe pros and cons, address fears and challenges, and encourage folks to experiment and learn. We often challenge ourselves with the following question, **what can we do to eliminate the fear that often prevents folks from getting to the excitement of learning?**

We don't always have the answers, but even when we do, we are trained to facilitate impactful sessions leading folks to find their answers, and possible solutions to whatever pain points they need to tackle.

As a leader, coach, and digital transformation consultant with over a decade of experience, I like to use an "imaginary wand" exercise to encourage folks to look beyond any limiting beliefs regarding their organizations, processes, innovation, ideas, and often their growth opportunities. The exercise consists of one question: "If you had a magic wand and there were no obstacles of any sort, what changes would you make?"

Throughout the book, as different stories are shared to educate and inspire, the intent is to extract lessons from a challenge that either myself or one of the contributing authors faced in the past and were able to learn from.

The book is not about succeeding or failing; it is about **Facing Yet Another Important Lesson (FYAIL)**. It is about exploring limiting beliefs, resolving

Introduction

conflict, achieving organizational alignment, leveraging resistance, measuring what matters, mastering accountability, and maximizing the value delivered. We share what contributes to success, but we primarily look at it all as a learning opportunity.

While the similarities between the digital transformation world and Hogwarts abound, this book is intended to bring you real-life lessons — no witchcraft or wizardry!

The stories in this book are written to share experiences, educate, and inspire. They're here to encourage and reinforce the idea that when we replace the fear of failing with the excitement of learning, we have a much better chance of succeeding in digital transformations — and so much more in life.

Illustration a. What this book is about

What is Digital Transformation?

"One of the most important things to understand is that digital transformation is not a one size fits all solution — every company should decide what digital transformation means to them. Digital transformation is not about technology; It is opportunity or problem-driven. It is about enabling business goals and outcomes and not the technology. Technology is the means to the end. Technologies provide possibilities for efficiencies and customer-centricity, but if the organization lacks the right mindset to change and current organizational practices are flawed, digital transformation will magnify those flaws.

Digital transformation is having a simple, scalable, and flexible digital infrastructure to serve the business effectively.

Corporate vision and alignment of strategic goals to this vision is required before any investments are made. Ultimately, digital transformation is about applying technology in the right places in order to achieve specific business goals. Those goals can be internal and external. Ability to provide customers with proper and timely support could be an external goal, but improving the efficiency of the internal processes could be that internal goal that can make the external goal accomplishable.

Digital transformation should be tied to business results such as customer satisfaction, productivity, time to market, innovation, cost reduction, and compliance."

Tatiana Thomas
Director of Customer Experience and
Digital Strategy | Contributing Author

"Transformations are large-scale changes that typically involve rethinking entire businesses or large parts of them. These can affect hundreds or thousands of employees and will usually touch people, processes, and tools. It makes it essential for success that the people planning and executing the change consider the impact this will have and employ strategies that will help with adoption. Examples of common transformations today include:

- *Agile: adopting the mindsets and methods to become more responsive and faster at releasing solutions*
- *Cloud: moving a company's apps, processes, data to the cloud in order to take advantage of cost savings and allow for more rapid scaling*
- *Digital: when companies move more parts of the organization to digital technologies to meet changing market needs"*

Jennifer Greve
Transformation Specialist | Contributing Author

What is Agile Transformation?

"Agile transformation is a change in culture to support a new way of working. That means everyone will be touched by this change in an organization to be sustainable long-term. From individual contributors to the CEO, all play a significant role in a successful Agile transformation and the organization's resiliency to handle the opportunities and challenges of the future."

Naomi Kent
Transformation Specialist | Contributing Author

"Digital transformation is about technology and business partnering to deliver amazing experiences to their internal and external customers with **agile mindset and culture** to aid the transformation and make it a successful journey where one cannot be without the other."

Natalie Vinitsky
Dynamic Change Agent | Contributing Author

"Agile transformation begins with the change in mindset to build and deliver solutions to the customers. It's not adopting one particular process or tool, but the company ecosystem needs to embrace the agile mindset.

For example, if the SDLC (Software Development Lifecycle) is updated now to use agile methodology, but the company finance processes are not revised, the outcome of the transformation will not be very effective."

Asmita Dharap
Senior Manager Software Quality | Contributing Author

What are Limiting Beliefs?

"Limiting beliefs are thoughts and opinions we hold about ourselves that prevent us from challenging ourselves and growing. Henry Ford once said, "Whether you think you can, or you think you can't - you're right." They are easy to develop but hard to remove. Most times, they are subconscious thoughts that guide our behaviors. Recognizing them in yours and others helps to remove the barriers they create. Facing your limiting beliefs and actively pursuing a growth mindset will be key to your 'FYAIL'ing."

Jennifer Clarke-Burke
Agilist | Contributing Author

"Limiting beliefs starts with an individual who often doubts their own ability or experience and therefore projects that limiting belief to a problem at hand. What is the best way to eliminate limiting beliefs? Is it to take a leap of faith, experiment, and try a new approach even if it has not been done before? It starts with reframing your limiting belief within yourself. If you try a new

approach, it will fail because we have not figured out details, we have not discussed all valuables. But what if it will succeed? What if your new mantra was "you have nothing to lose and everything to gain!" How can you reframe your mindset and outlook for expected results with that new mantra? Look for a trusted partner, mentor, advisor, or even an executive coach whose sound coaching and guidance will help you reframe and start to believe in a possibility of a new and different outcome. You can start to believe in yourself again when people you trust believe in you first."

Alina Aronova
Executive Coach | Digital Transformation Expert | Contributing Author

"One of the most common limiting beliefs in digital transformations is "this change cannot be done here because we have always worked a certain way." People tend to underestimate the power of deliberate, well-thought-out, systemic enterprise change management. Settling for the status quo is the path of least resistance and requires no effort. One of the jobs of a transformation leader or an enterprise coach is to help people see what is on the other side of a transformation and why it is worth the effort and the discomfort. Change is possible; it just depends on how bad you want it."

Nadia Clifford
Agilist | Technology Delivery Leader | Contributing Author

CHAPTER 1

Limiting Beliefs

Illustration 1a. Limiting Beliefs

About the Stories in this Chapter

"Your time is limited, so don't waste it living someone else's life. Don't be trapped by dogma - which is living with the results of other people's thinking. Don't let the noise of others' opinions drown out your own inner voice. And most important, have the courage to follow your heart and intuition. They somehow already know what you truly want to become. Everything else is secondary."

—STEVE JOBS

It is truly remarkable when our hearts and intuition know what we truly want to become. But what happens when our inner voice, our heart, and our intuition turn on us and tell us, not to even bother trying? What happens when we turn a blind eye to things that we could, in fact, accomplish?

In my memoir *Life Worth Living*, I share my journey of enrolling in Northeastern's computer science program, doubting that it was something I could even accomplish.

My self-doubt started at the age of seven, when a teacher casually compared me to my brilliant sister, implying that I wasn't quite on par with her in the intelligence department. Prior to coming to the US in 1992, neither myself nor anyone in my family thought going to college was a possibility for me. Impeccable soft skills weren't valued that much back in the USSR, and since I wasn't considered the brightest kid on the block, any expectations for my future career were set very low.

Things changed after coming to the US, during my freshman year in high school. All of a sudden, all my friends were planning to go to college and while most of the classes I had taken were dance, my GPA was decent enough to apply. So, I applied, got accepted, graduated, and became a software engineer, despite my lack of faith in myself.

Moments of doubt when it came to becoming a software engineer, a manager, a leader, a consultant, an independent consultant, attempting sales, or becoming a business owner would keep coming back each time a new opportunity was on the horizon. Still, the doubt faded away each time, replacing it with a story of learning, overcoming fears, and even succeeding. The stories shared in this chapter, written from the perspective of the main character, Vita, are the journey of facing each of those learning opportunities and overcoming doubt along the way. For the most part, Vita is based on myself, with journeys and doubts similar to my own. Halfway through this chapter, when Vita finally recognizes that not everything that comes naturally to her is as easy for other people, the story concludes with the following, "As a mentor for others, one of Vita's passions became helping people find their unique trait, their gift, their 'core genius,' a concept considered to be your natural talent, the area in which you shine." We all have it. We just need to find our own.

In these pages, there is also a story about the value of a mentor. Finding a mentor, someone who can help differentiate if your doubts are legitimate or are simply just limiting beliefs is key to succeeding at anything you set your mind to!

This chapter is concluded with a section on limiting beliefs when it comes to digital transformations! Just like in our own careers, we often doubt

Limiting Beliefs

that something can be accomplished in our organizations. Although some challenges may be legitimate, it is also often a case that our limiting beliefs in what we can truly accomplish stand in the way of even trying.

Illustration 1b: Getting comfortable being uncomfortable leads to desired outcomes

1.1 Becoming a Digital Transformation Coach

Sharing her career journey for the purpose of inspiring, educating, and helping someone choose their own path has been a passion of Vita's for years now. She realized just how much she enjoyed it when she became a hiring manager for the first time. She chose to balance her team with folks who were more experienced than her, as well as those who were just starting out. She appreciated learning and was at a point in her career where coaching and mentoring others felt right.

It had been a few years since Vita had any formal human resource (HR) responsibilities, but the passion for sharing knowledge and experience was stronger than ever. So, she enrolled in a formal program for women in the high-tech world to become a mentor. The program matched mentors with those who were looking to learn and get inspired.

Shortly after, she got on a phone call with a woman named Julie she met at the Women in Tech program.

"Hi! Nice to hear from you," Vita said, answering her cell phone. "I will be honest with you, after I read your experience and credentials on LinkedIn, I wasn't sure I could be of any help. But I am happy to share whatever I know."

"Oh, I thought this was a perfect match!" Julie replied. "I have been in the military for 20 years and regardless of my job title currently, I feel like I don't really know much about the corporate world. I would love to learn what roles there are and what skills are required. I need to figure out a path forward after retiring from the military, so anything you can share will be helpful. To start, I would love to understand what you do as a **digital transformation coach**? Is it different from an **agile coach**? I also hear the roles of a **scrum master** and a **product owner** come up pretty often. I would love to understand if maybe one of these roles could be something for me. I know we only have an hour at the moment, but I would also love to learn how you actually got to your current role! Did you have to get a certain certification or a degree?"

Vita dove into the details, pausing periodically to make sure Julie was still with her. Since Julie consistently showed signs that she was not only following but interested, Vita shared the whole story of her career journey.

> "Sure, I can definitely talk about these roles and share my life journey!" Vita replied.
>
> She began by sharing the fact that she only recently became a digital transformation coach, working for a consulting company. She was part of a team of different experts who would go in and look at a client company overall, from **company vision** and their **roadmap,** to how their teams are structured, their **infrastructure**, their incentive programs, and anything else that would help an organization compete in this fast-changing world.
>
> Vita shared that her role often depended on what an organization needed. Since her expertise is in agile coaching on all levels of an organization, as well as training and facilitation, she had trained over 700 people on **agile methodology, scrum,** and **kanban frameworks**, as well as facilitated large planning sessions with many teams.
>
> Vita also shared that for a different client, she and her colleagues had delivered leadership training. After Vita and the team listened

to the client's pain points and proposed various topics, the client chose to focus on decision making, empowering people, easing up on command and control, listening skills, and conflict resolution.

"When it comes to digital transformation," Vita said, "leaders play a huge role. Besides a clear vision, organizational alignment, growth mindset, and culture, they are also on the hook to lead by example when it comes to behavior. That's what enterprise and executive coaches often focus on. Overall, we do what needs to get done!

As I mentioned, digital transformation coach is a relatively recent role for me. I started out as a software engineer. After that, I worked in customer support, then as a QA automation engineer, I then became a scrum master, the role you said you heard so much about. It was purely a coincidence for me. I wasn't looking to become a scrum master, but I eventually took a new job and started working as one full-time. First, I had to learn the scrum framework. Eventually, I worked with product owners, who come up with a vision for the product and break down the requirements so that the developers could develop and test small chunks of work in short periods of time.

Scrum masters facilitate different ceremonies (aka meetings) of the scrum framework and their primary job is to remove impediments, so the team can operate in the most efficient and effective way. At some point, I got a chance to hire a team of scrum masters and agile coaches and learned a ton from them. Then I got a chance to do that again at a different company. It has been a pretty amazing journey I have to admit. As far as certification and degrees, honestly, a path to becoming a scrum master and then an agile coach can be very different. Many of the scrum masters I had hired had a ton of different certifications. I never personally felt the need, but I know for many, it had helped to get a foot in the door. Some companies look for scrum masters who are very technical but there are actually pros and cons in that approach. Probably a longer discussion for another day."

"Wow, thank you so much for sharing! That's a pretty amazing journey and you sound so passionate about the work you do!" Julie said.

"I enjoy what I do, yes. So, was there anything I mentioned that was appealing to you? What are some of the things you currently do in your job that excite you?" Vita asked.

As Julie shared the specifics of her current role and they discussed whether a role of a scrum master or a product owner would be a good fit for Julie, Vita couldn't help but recall with a smile some of the details of how she took a leap of faith (taking a new job, feeling she didn't qualify for the job at all) and how her journey had begun over a decade ago. Many times, since that moment, she was faced with a new opportunity and considered it right away, knowing that any doubt she may have had was nothing but a limiting belief.

1.2 Getting Comfortable Being Uncomfortable

This concept of getting comfortable being uncomfortable immediately resonated with Vita when she read the book, *The Innovation Stack: Building an Unbeatable Business, One Crazy Idea at a Time* by Jim McKelvey, co-founder of Square. Vita chose this concept over the idea of "getting out of your comfort zone" because it made more sense to her personally. There is a difference between pushing yourself to do something that you don't feel comfortable doing and actually embracing the fact that it is ok to be uncomfortable. Once you get comfortable being uncomfortable, there is no need to force yourself to do anything. You just take one step at a time doing what needs to get done, knowing that it will eventually get you to your desired outcome. No need to stress out, just business as usual. For Vita, it took decades of embracing those very uncomfortable moments that lead her to get comfortable being uncomfortable, and below is the story of how it started in the context of her leadership journey.

Mike and Vita met when Vita joined a small company as a **QA automation engineer**. There were only two engineering teams, a core team focusing on all the backend code and a UI team focusing on everything related to user interface. Vita was on the **core team**, while Mike managed the **UI team**. Vita had very little understanding of what **Agile** was all about at the time and even less about scrum and scrum roles. One morning, Vita learned that someone who worked in customer support and was a scrum master on Mike's team was leaving the company to pursue other opportunities.

"Hey, Vita, I had this thought," said Mike when Vita stopped by his office to discuss a software bug. "I wanted to ask if you would be interested in being a scrum master on my team."

"A scrum who?" she asked.

"A scrum master," Mike laughed. "You would be great at it!"

"What does a scrum master do?" Vita was game for anything, but she had never heard this odd-sounding job title before, so she wanted to know what it was that she would potentially be good at.

"As a scrum master, you facilitate all the scrum ceremonies and remove impediments so the team can be more efficient. Here, take a look at this training guide from Jeff Sutherland," Mike suggested, handing Vita over a binder. "We all got trained and certified recently by him and he is one of the guys who started Scrum!"

"Sure, thanks!" Vita replied. "I will take a look and we can chat more about it tomorrow!"

Fast forward three years, Mike and Vita were having lunch at the fanciest restaurant Vita had ever eaten at after Vita just finished a presentation on "Agile 101" at Mike's new company.

"Wow! That was amazing! Who did you tell them I was?! It felt like I was a celebrity of some kind, and they were about to roll out the red carpet in front of me!" Vita inhaled some air, taking a break from the outburst of emotions long enough for her friend Mike to answer.

"I told them the truth, that you are the best for this job," he replied with a smile.

Limiting Beliefs

"I am not sure about that... But the presentation went well! Nobody threw tomatoes or raw eggs at me!" Vita laughed. "I had my bar set very low, so I wouldn't get disappointed."

"I have told you many times already and I will say it again, this company needs you and I hope you would consider at least coming in for an interview," Mike insisted. He had been trying for two months now to persuade Vita to interview for the company he recently joined. Mike has been trying different persuasion techniques, from being super nice telling her the company desperately needed someone like her, to saying something along the lines, "Fine, go ahead and do nothing about your career."

They finally agreed that perhaps a "Lunch & Learn" presentation on a Friday would be something Vita could commit to.

That's where the unbelievable journey of Vita's career would soon begin.

She was immediately wowed by the water fountain in the lobby, the elevator that automatically, without her pushing any buttons inside, took her to the top floor. She was impressed by the glass door conference rooms overlooking Boston Tea Party Museum, by the people greeting her like she was a known celebrity, by a guy putting a microphone on her before the presentation as if she was this big shot public speaker, by the questions people asked and by the appreciation they expressed for her coming.

Mike's persuasion techniques worked after all. A month after delivering the presentation and agreeing to come in for an interview, Vita took a leap of faith and joined the new company as a full-time scrum master, embracing a leadership role and leaving behind the days of being a hands-on engineer. The fact that she didn't qualify for the job was not a limiting belief in this case. She really did not qualify for it. The fact that she doubted she could do the job because she knew little, that was a limiting belief! She would only truly realize it years later when she would reflect on just how little she knew about scrum and about agile in general. She would realize she had zero knowledge about **scaling** or any of the **scaling frameworks**. In fact, she didn't even know what the word "framework" was!

However, she would also realize that being comfortable knowing that you know very little about a topic or a challenge you are faced with and hiring people who know more than you, allows you to bring a lot of value to the organization and the people you work with. Vita realized that the reason Mike wanted her at the new company was that he saw how willing and eager she was to learn and face challenges. When she first became a scrum master and didn't know anything about the role, she read many books and continuously experimented with a physical scrum board, improving it **sprint by sprint** until the team agreed it made them a lot more efficient. She had done the same later on with virtual tools and anything else she needed to learn to become better at her job. Having a **growth mindset** and believing your talents can be developed through hard work and input from others allows you to achieve more than you could imagine.

1.3 Becoming a Manager

"Go ahead and start hiring," said Vita's manager at the time, the vice president of engineering.

"You mean you want new scrum masters to report directly to me?" she had to clarify.

"Is there anyone else who might be a better candidate?" he replied.

"I don't know…" Vita said, sounding very unsure and uncomfortable, thinking they could potentially report to him. But her manager already had a few directors of engineering reporting to him. It could be that he didn't want any additional employees he would have to write reviews for at the end of the year. Perhaps, he truly thought Vita would be the best candidate for the job, we will never know. But this is how Vita became a manager for the first time.

Vita's very first hire was a no-brainer. She had absolutely no doubt that he was an amazing candidate. She phone screened and interviewed potential candidates non-stop all week and was losing all hope until she spoke to Tom. She was sitting in the parking lot of her kids' dance studio waiting for their lessons to finish, dialing yet again a phone number and embracing herself for disappointment. She was not sure why the phone screening wasn't going well. She never considered herself a tough interviewer. She was just looking for people who had a bit of energy and knew more than she did. She knew she was in over her head with this job and so she looked for candidates she could partner with and learn from. Vita's current colleagues seemed to know even less about agile and different frameworks that would help scale an organization poised to grow by 200 engineers in one year. Later on, they would hire more leaders that knew Agile and how to scale, but that would be later on.

Vita was given an opportunity to learn and grow and although it was out of her comfort zone and she did feel very uncomfortable, she knew she could pull it off if she hired the right people. Thankfully, a phone interview with Tom was far from disappointing. Tom was amazing. He knew so much and talking to him gave Vita a lot of hope. Vita knew she wanted to hire him after their 30-minute conversation. Now she just had to persuade Tom the company was doing well, and that she would be great to work for. Tom would have to relocate so it had to be worth it for him. Tom was living in a different state at the time and they didn't meet until he moved to Boston and came in for his first day. Vita didn't have any experience hiring or managing. It was all based on her intuition and hiring Tom was definitely beginner's luck!

Reflecting back, Vita often thought about how she never wanted to be a manager. She didn't think she would be a great one and cringed every time someone on her team called her "boss." Her biggest fear in becoming a manager was having to fire someone, and she was pretty sure she wouldn't have the guts. A time came when she had to. To this day, firing someone is one of the worst experiences she had to go through, but it allowed her to grow and realize that even when faced with a difficult interpersonal situation, one can still be civil. When you treat people with empathy and respect, you may stay friends for years to come. She had learned that her natural desire to help others, empathy, ability to collaborate, communicate, and lead by example when it came to a growth mindset, were some of the main skills needed to be a great manager. She also learned that even when you feel extremely uncomfortable at a particular moment, it is ok. Although nobody still knows for sure where the phrase "This too shall pass" originated from, it has been Vita's long-term favorite!

1.4 Getting a Mentor

The newly hired chief technology officer (CTO) of the company came up to Vita and said, "Whatever it is you are doing with the teams here, can you also please do it in our India office?"

Apparently, having work estimated in a tool called Jira, which allowed her to generate some basic reports, was enough to impress the new leadership team. Transparency wasn't established yet among the engineering teams and the few things Vita helped to put in place were bringing enough value for the leadership to desire more of it.

It was flattering to Vita but there was a dilemma. Vita had small children and for her, even taking this job in Boston and having to commute by train — which turned out to be unreliable and took over an hour — was a stretch for her family. Vita needed to hire someone who would be willing to travel to India.

That is where Keira came in. Beginner's luck (or at least that's what Vita called it) in hiring continued with her second hire as well! A woman around Vita's age named Keira, who came in to interview for a different position, ended up meeting with Vita instead for a coaching role. Keira turned out to be a peer who Vita learned from over the years and who she could rely on many different occasions in their coaching and leadership journey together. Keira ended up being one of Vita's most impactful mentors who contributed to the success of her agile coaching and leadership career at every step of the way.

"What can I do to help?" Vita asked Keira.

"It would help if you introduced me to the right people in the India office," Keira answered.

"You got it! I plan to travel there a couple of days before your arrival, meet as many people as I can and let them know ahead of time the fact that you are coming, the purpose of the trip, and the desired outcome from this engagement," Vita shared her plan.

"Thank you! That will make a huge difference!" Keira noted.

The result from that trip to India was exactly as Vita and Kiera had hoped. Connections were made and desired outcomes were achieved. Keira always shared what she was accomplishing in the India office and through those conversations, Vita learned just how much more there is to learn about scaling organizations, **change management,** and coaching in general.

Although it was Vita's job as a manager and a Leader to make sure Keira had everything she needed to succeed at her job, it was Kiera who in fact became Vita's mentor. Mentors don't have to be your managers. Consider the relationship a partnership, where you learn from each other.

> Two years later, after Vita moved on to another company, Keira would continue to educate Vita. It is Keira who mentioned to Vita one night, while they were walking around Boston after work, about an event called **program increment planning.** It was a two-day planning session with a specific agenda focusing on a specific outcome, which sounded like a perfect solution to a problem Vita shared with Keira. Keira explained that this planning session comes from the **Scaled Agile Framework (SAFe)** and is used widely in the industry. Somehow, Vita hadn't heard of it before. It sounded like the best thing since sliced bread, and she

couldn't wait to experiment with it. Eventually, it would be Keira who ran the first experiment at Vita's new company after Vita finally persuaded Keira to join her there. Vita couldn't imagine facilitating such a big event herself, not until she had observed Keira doing it a few times. It was yet another limiting belief on Vita's part, doubting she had it in her to do something of this scale. It was Keira once again, who through coaching, mentoring, and guiding, persuaded Vita to give it a shot, willing to be there for any support Vita would need.

Eventually, Vita would end up not only facilitating these large-scale program increment planning sessions for hundreds of teams at different companies, but she would also end up teaching workshops and training others to do it effectively.

What makes mentors such valuable people in one's career and life? Mentors are a strong source of knowledge who can give you a specific insight to solve a pain point you are facing just in time, so you are more likely to consume the information they are giving you. Mentors offer encouragement, help you set goals, and be accountable to achieve them. They are key people who can help differentiate if your doubts are real and you truly need additional help, or they are simply just limiting beliefs!

1.5 Becoming a Consultant

"I don't think I could be a consultant," said one of Vita's former colleagues in a virtual coffee meeting over zoom.

"What makes you say that?" Vita asked, although she could very well guess most of the reasons since she herself had made that statement prior to actually becoming one.

"Well, it is the instability of the job, not having 401K, no vacation days," the colleague paused.

"It might be true in some cases, but I am actually a full-time employee, so there is a 401K and vacation!" Vita offered.

"Wait, are you not an independent consultant working for yourself?" her colleague asked.

"Not yet, but that could be in the future as well! At the moment, I work full-time for a consulting company," Vita clarified.

"Are you guaranteed a job though? In general, what are the pros of being a consultant? Don't you have to go from one engagement to another and start from scratch each time, proving yourself and meeting new people all the time?" the colleague said it as if it was the worst thing in the world, which made Vita laugh.

"Everything you just mentioned is what I love about consulting!" Vita replied, still laughing. "I get to meet new people. I get to learn new things. And if I am lucky, I also get to be a change architect, meaning I get to be creative and come up with the best way to actually solve whatever pain points they need to address. The moment it is no longer a challenge, I get to go to another client and start all over. For the most part, it is not different from a full-time job, except you don't stay at the same engagement for a long period of time. So far it has been nine months at most. Sounds good, doesn't it?"

"Oh, I don't know. I suppose you are right. It does sound like you love your job. Are you worried about not having a job between engagements though? That would make me really uncomfortable."

"Honestly, when I took my first consulting job, I figured I had nothing to lose. I happened to work myself out of the last full-time job I had and when we decided it was time for me to move on, I had a month's notice plus a severance package. I was actually going to take a few months off, but this consulting job landed on my lap pretty much a week later. My thought process was that if it doesn't work out, I can always look for a full-time job then. It has been a few years now and I've never looked back," Vita said again with a smile. "You just never know. We tend to have some preconceived notions about certain things but unless we try, there is no way to predict if it will work out. Honestly, even with full-time employment, you never know. So, I tend to leave the worrying until I cross that bridge."

"That's a great attitude!" said the colleague. "It is always nice to talk to you Vita. Somehow, I always leave our conversations inspired and at ease that all will be well."

A few weeks later, when someone asked Vita how she managed her time in order to get everything done, she had to really think about it. She used to think that if she could be a consultant on multiple engagements, then anyone could. She thought that if she could manage a full-time job and say, write a book, then anyone could. She didn't think it was a big deal to constantly meet new people and get used to new work environments, but eventually, she realized that it was a big deal for many.

Consulting worked for her because she loved meeting new people and learning new environments. Although if she thought back, there were plenty of times where that would make her very uncomfortable, but not anymore. She was comfortable being uncomfortable and saw it as a fun challenge to prove each time to a new client that she knew what she was talking about. Her biggest lesson was to stop assuming that because she could do something and loved doing it, it would work for everyone. She had to learn to give herself some credit that not only did she have certain unique personality traits that were an advantage in consulting, but she was an action taker and got things done. She also had a natural talent for connecting with people. As a mentor for others, one of Vita's passions became helping people find their unique trait, their gift, their "core genius," a concept considered to be your natural talent, the area in which you shine.

1.6 Becoming an Independent Consultant/Business Owner

"We are looking for a very light touch engagement," John said.

John was introduced to Vita by a former colleague who was a senior software developer and was in Vita's training on agile and scrum years ago. Her colleague now worked for a small startup where John was the VP of engineering and they were looking for someone to be a fly on the wall during their scrum ceremonies and to recommend things they could improve.

"OK, can you tell me a bit more about what type of pain points you are trying to solve?" Vita asked.

"Well, we've been embracing Scrum for a while now and teams are doing a great job, but I think we might have reached a plateau. We value continuous improvement and figure someone from the outside, someone with your expertise could perhaps see gaps in the way we operate." John offered.

"I hear you. Well, let me tell you a bit about what I do and where I work and what this engagement could potentially look like," Vita said. "I work full time for a consulting company. We work as a team of experts, from agile coaches to **UX designers**, from former **CIOs** to **DevOps** experts, change management experts with degrees in organizational psychology, really anything a company might potentially need to solve a problem in their digital or agile transformation on all levels of an organization."

"This sounds really amazing but also very expensive. Listen, I will be honest with you, we are not looking for anything big that would cost millions. We are really looking for a very light touch engagement," John sounded like many folks who had a certain perception, perhaps a bad experience, engaging a large consulting firm.

"Oh, it can be a very light touch engagement," Vita replied confidently. "For example, based on my current availability, we could say 20% of my time is dedicated to you for a 3-month engagement. You only engage with me and pay accordingly, NOT millions, but what you get, in reality, is also all the experts who support me behind the scenes. We pick a day that is dedicated to you, and I build the rest of my schedule around that. If, for some reason, I am not able to get something done, one of my colleagues could jump in so we don't lose time. It really does work well."

Vita had done her best to show the value they would receive if they engaged through the consulting company, but she could tell John was getting slightly disappointed because he was hoping to hire Vita directly.

"Here is another option," Vita continued. "I did recently register my own Limited Liability Company (LLC), but it is a public speaking business only. So, no fancy training slides on agile or scrum. That I do through the consulting company only. What I offer as part of my business is a series of keynotes over a 6-month period. This doesn't mean that I can't answer any questions you may have. I won't be able to observe the teams as much but to better prepare for a keynote, I do like to be a fly on the wall for a meeting or two just to get a sense of the interaction and company environment. Not all keynotes are custom, and I tend to speak for 30 minutes and leave 30 minutes for Q&A so I can answer any specific questions folks may have."

Vita noticed the excitement on John's face. He was all smiles and said with a lot of enthusiasm that he would prefer to start with the second option, where Vita delivers the keynotes and gets to know the team members. After that, the 20% through the consulting company actually sounded like a good option as well. Thus, without much thought, Vita acted as a salesperson for both her own company as well as the consulting company she worked for. She found a way to describe two potential solutions and let the customer decide what would be the most valuable for them.

This was the first time Vita mentioned her newly registered **LLC, RALM3 Consulting**, to a real potential client. A year prior, when she was writing her memoir and her publishing coach, who also happened to be a business coach, kept talking about owning a business, Vita insisted that it wasn't for her. Vita had a well-paying full-time job in the world of technology. Why would she own a business, with all the hassle of finding clients and trying to sell them something (another preconceived notion that selling means bugging people rather than solving a problem for them, which Vita would overcome eventually!). However, the seeds that had been planted a year prior were slowly turning into reality for Vita. After all, owning a business is providing value to someone. It is all about solving a problem or pain point. It can really be anything you want it to be and if at the moment, delivering four keynotes over a period of six months was all Vita could do, then that's what it would be. Vita found a way to continue working full-time at the job she loved, but at the same time get her feet wet in the world of entrepreneurship.

1.7 Getting Over the Fear of Being a Salesperson

When thinking about the topic of limiting beliefs, Vita often thought about how, at first, she didn't think she could be an engineer, then she didn't think she would be a good manager, then she thought consulting wouldn't be a good fit. She also didn't think she could ever be a business owner, not to mention a salesperson! She even offended someone once when she said she wouldn't be a good salesperson because she couldn't lie! Vita to this day could remember the expression on the guy's face. He eventually recovered and answered, "Salespeople don't lie, they help customers."

Vita was an engineer at that point and for whatever reason had this major misconception about sales engraved in her brain. She wasn't sure where it came from, but it was strong.

A decade later, she still felt ashamed about that comment. What a horrible thing to say, especially since it was her boss's boss who offered her a job within his sales team and was sure she would be perfect for it. Vita hoped there was a 10-year statute of limitations when it came to saying stupid things.

Over the years, when Vita shifted her mindset and understood that being a salesperson is actually bringing solutions to clients and solving their pain points, she was in fact ready to become a salesperson and a business owner herself!

1.8 Business Owner vs. Entrepreneur

To decompress after a long day, Vita opened Facebook and noticed a LIVE stream in progress. It was a show hosted weekly by RUSSIANBOSTON.TV, which covers topics varying from overview of all social events in Boston to more serious topics like medical care, entrepreneurship, and even politics. This particular episode had a guest who was so inspiring, Vita reached out to her right away to see if she would be interested in collaborating. Her name was Victoria and she agreed to meet over zoom.

"Victoria! Great job on the show! I truly enjoyed it and could relate to many things you mentioned," Vita said.

"Thank you for reaching out, Vita! I appreciate the kind words. I would love to interview with you and contribute to the book you are writing, I am honored!" said Victoria.

"Absolutely! You have so much wisdom, and you said so many things that are relevant to the first chapter of the book, which is all about limiting beliefs. Before we get there, though, let me show you, in general, what the book is about, and you can decide the extent to which you would like to contribute."

"Sure, let's do it!" Victoria replied.

Victoria's energy was through the roof. It was infectious and inspired Vita to engage with Victoria for collaboration. Of course, Victoria had impressive credentials too. A bachelor's degree in computer science from Cornell, an MBA from Columbia, an executive role on Wall Street, as well as a slew of other impressive accomplishments. But it was Victoria's energy and passion for her business that made Vita want to reach out.

"Can you explain the difference between **business owners** and **entrepreneurs**? I am curious to understand if I would engage your services as a small business owner who isn't looking to raise money per se, but needs help producing a financial model for my business?" Vita asked Victoria.

"Every business owner is an entrepreneur. The difference, I think, lies in your goals and growth potential. The founder of Facebook is an entrepreneur, but an owner of a dry-cleaning business is a business owner. However, they both deal with similar challenges, just on a different scale. If a dry-cleaning business grows into a nationwide network and goes public, suddenly the owner is an entrepreneur because they scaled the business. If we switch a dry-cleaning business to a fast-food restaurant, we have several examples of that: McDonald's, Wendy's, and Burger King."

"I see the small nuance but not too much of a difference between the two, to be honest. In any case," Vita continued with a smile, "how do you collaborate with executives (both business owners and entrepreneurs)?"

"The way I collaborate with executives is similar across the board," Victoria replied. "For example, a startup founder may ask me, 'How do I make $100M in five years?' A business owner may ask me, 'How do I triple my revenue?' The process is the same. You build a plan that connects strategic decisions to financial results and implement monitoring systems to ensure effectiveness. That's what I call **strategic financial modeling**, which is our expertise. This way, financial models become your business intelligence tools which empower you to make better business decisions and respond more intelligently to market feedback."

"What are some of the limiting beliefs that you see your clients have when they come to you for advice?" Vita asked.

Limiting Beliefs

"Right. Well, I have written a lot on this topic. So, let me send you some of the reflections that I have gathered over the years since I believe they would be very applicable here," Victoria offered.

Within seconds, Vita was looking through a ton of writing like a kid in a candy store. Vita paused at the following content on "limiting beliefs" that Victoria had written,

"If you can dream it, you can do it." - Walt Disney

Today I've been thinking about how we should all dream big. Nothing is impossible if you believe in it and work hard.

Like one of the entrepreneurs from the The Startup Station's clubhouse said:

"If Elon Musk can dream of colonizing Mars and be well on the way to doing it, anything that we do here on Earth should be a piece of cake."

I see so many entrepreneurs setting meager goals. They don't realize that by doing it, they are selling their dream short. You will never achieve it if you don't even try to shoot for the stars or don't think about how you will get there. The only limits which exist are the ones we create ourselves. We decide what is possible. We determine what we can do.

As Vita browsed through the folder Vitoria shared with her, she came across something else that was very relevant to what the acronym FYAIL (Facing Yet Another Important Lesson) stands for,

Failure is an intrinsic part of entrepreneurship. Can we deal with it effectively? How do we not let it define who we are, what our purpose is? Where can we get the strength and confidence to go on after everything crashes?

*One of the entrepreneurs I've been talking to at The Startup Station's clubhouse said something which stuck with me: "**It's only a failure if we don't learn from it.**"*

I thought that it was a brilliant insight and a complete shift in perspective. We all go through ups and downs. The ups make us feel like we are kings of the world. The downs - well, those are the ones from which it can be hard to recover. But, if everything is a learning opportunity, then any "down" becomes just one of the outcomes that might have happened. Although mainly it becomes a source of info which we must use to change direction.

Dreaming big and not being afraid of failure, what a great message, Vita thought to herself. She was glad she reached out to Victoria. She met someone who, in addition to being an extremely accomplished and interesting person, shared with Vita many interests, values, and beliefs. Vita also thought about how small steps, small actions such as reaching out to someone she didn't know on LinkedIn, led to this significant contribution to her book and future collaboration. Vita often spoke about the importance of taking action, and, in this case, she again proved the significance of practicing what she preached!

1.9 Becoming a Board Member

Vita heard about the position of a board member in her 40s. When she first heard the term from someone at a conference, she recalled a few other instances where it came up in conversations and realized that she didn't know much about it. When she asked a new acquaintance to share some of her experiences, Vita started thinking how cool it would be to be a board member. However, she immediately brushed off the idea thinking, *who am I and what have I accomplished, really?*

A few months went by, and she started seeing a few postings here and there on LinkedIn for board member positions. She wondered how she had never noticed them before. She pinged Liz, the woman she had met at the conference, to ask for advice and if it was worth reaching out about the positions. She learned that companies normally don't look for board members advertising on LinkedIn. Normally folks who want you to be their board member seek you out if they think you are a good fit.

Vita then asked a very specific question that had been on her mind for a few months now, "How do you know that you are actually good enough to be a board member?"

"Are we talking about **imposter syndrome**?" Liz laughed.

"Either imposter syndrome or legitimate lack of qualifications," Vita replied with a smile.

"Well, I can think of a few reasons which would cause one to feel like an imposter based on my experience," said Liz.

"Please! I would love to hear those! Hopefully followed by you sharing how one could get rid of that feeling!"

"Sure, I can give it a shot!" Liz said. "I think the first false belief is that most board members come from private equity, venture capital, investment, and banking backgrounds. That's just not true."

Vita didn't say anything, eager to learn more.

"Then, there is a belief that you must understand every little nuance of the business and its finances. A belief that other operational executives who land corporate board roles must have more knowledge and experience than you have. A belief that all your professional experiences are still not good enough for the role you are expected to play and the insights you are expected to provide must be no less than brilliant."

"Do you think those are general beliefs or more specific to those who are in general perfectionists and have very high expectations for themselves?" Vita asked.

"Ha! Good point! Well, I can only share my personal observations and experiences from my colleagues who are board members. Who, now that you mentioned it, yes, all have that same quality of having very high expectations of themselves and others."

"Seriously though, how much of an expert do you have to be?" Vita continued.

Limiting Beliefs

"Well, at first I had this perception that I'd have to be an instantaneous expert for any technical question in any technical discipline, but I realized quickly that it is ok to say, 'I will get back to you.' We all know that no human being can know everything, and you will not get fired just because you didn't know something on the spot."

"And if you do not know everything there is the challenge to discover new things and better approaches, right? Do you have to be an expert in a specific industry to be a board member?"

"Interesting you ask. So, another common belief is that because you are not a specific industry expert you cannot ask insightful questions which will lead to 'aha' moments for the company's leadership team. You can and I have had great success with that. Your experience from a different industry can still be very relevant, transferable, and impactful or could provide a necessary and always lacking diversity of thought. "

"It does make a lot of sense," Vita said. Then asked if there was any advice that could be given to possibly manage and hopefully get rid of imposter syndrome.

"Acknowledge and vocalize your fear and have a frank conversation with people whose professional judgment you trust and respect. Seek out advice. Rely on the fact that someone else's reality is their perception, and it is a good thing. You could have public acknowledgment and monetary awards for your contribution from other board members coming your way as proof that they see and appreciate your impact while you might still feel insecure. Trust their reality in this case rather than yours. Finally, I would say engage a trusted executive coach who will help you work through the root of your imposter syndrome and help you define and implement tactics that will work for you. You might be experiencing imposter syndrome in other areas of your professional life or other leadership challenges that are worth tackling holistically and systematically."

"Thank you so much! That is really helpful!" Vita thanked Liz for such an insightful conversation. It had given her a lot of food for thought. Although she didn't necessarily feel strongly about pursuing a board member role, she was glad to gain that confidence that if someone did seek her out, she would at least consider it and be sure that her experience and expertise were plenty enough!

1.10 Limiting Beliefs in Digital Transformations

In the world of digital transformations, we often hear "It has always worked this way" or "It doesn't apply and won't work for us." As mentioned in the introduction of this book, our job as transformational leaders is to listen, understand, describe the pros and cons, address the fears and challenges, and encourage folks to experiment and to learn. It is also our job to differentiate what is a legitimate concern and what is simply a limiting belief. Although with enough experience, one can quickly differentiate reality from a limiting belief, it still takes time to get people to trust you and accept your help. Building trust and helping people address any fears or challenges in achieving their desired outcome is what the majority of this book is all about!

1.11 Exercise

Preparing for a Session with Your Mentor

1. List the responsibilities of your current role that you absolutely love doing

2. List three responsibilities of your current role that you would love to delegate

3. List one thing that you think or have been told you SHINE at

4. List one thing you can't imagine you would ever be able to do

5. If you had a magic wand and could grant any wish, what change(s) would you make in your organization or your career?

Illustration 1c. Most common limiting believe

CHAPTER 2

Resolving Conflict

Illustration 2a. Resolving Conflict

About the Stories in this Chapter

"If we manage conflict constructively, we harness its energy for creativity and development."

—KENNETH KAYE

Kenneth Kaye (January 24, 1946 – May 26, 2021) was an American psychologist and writer whose research, books, and articles connect the fields of human development, family relationships, and conflict resolution.

Have you noticed how even a minor conflict can drain so much energy out of you that you have a hard time focusing on anything productive? You end up replaying that conflict over and over and in the best-case scenario, you may self-reflect and extract a lesson or get to the root cause, but in the worst case, you just wasted brain cycles.

This chapter explores potential root causes, ways to prevent conflict, as well as ways to handle conflict if preventing it is no longer an option. We explore topics such as conflicting priorities and not being afraid of giving honest feedback; not following blindly but questioning if something doesn't feel right to you; having a habit of disagreeing for the sake of disagreeing; questioning your own emotional intelligence; and finally realizing how understanding your own communication style and the style of your peers may lead to better collaboration and in turn more successful outcomes. The chapter concludes by discussing common causes for conflict in digital transformations.

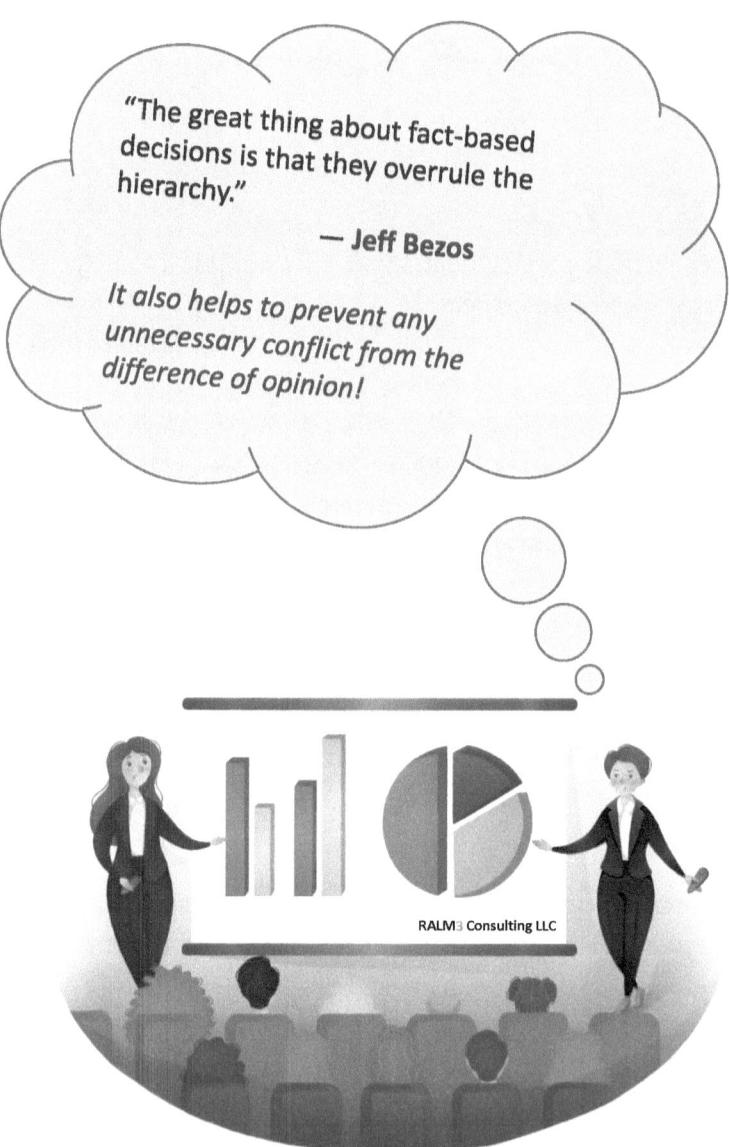

Illustration 2b. Fact based decisions help prevent conflict

2.1 When There Are Conflicting Priorities

It had been a while since Vita produced any software herself. Truth to be told, she never considered coding her core genius. She enjoyed being a software engineer and admits there was a thrill of the code compiling and doing what you intended it to do that was incomparable to any other role Vita has had since then. However, she mainly loved it for the interaction with team members and for the bragging rights it gave her among her non engineering friends, not because it was something she naturally shined at. That said, having the education and the experience of being a software engineer had allowed her to earn respect and connect with people on many levels in different business units of an organization throughout her career. That, along with curiosity, love for learning, and listening skills, which she did shine at, often put her in situations where folks whose hands were on the keyboard producing magic felt comfortable sharing their frustrations when stress led to steam coming out of their ears. Developers would often stop at her cubicle to just vent. At one point, the way her workspace was positioned, there was space in the corner for a small foam couch. She had bought it thinking she would ask for forgiveness and in the worst case, take it home, but it turned out to be everyone's favorite corner. One day, she came into the office and found a sign taped to the wall of her cubicle saying, "The Doctor is IN." It was funny and very fitting for that environment. The pattern of Vita listening to different causes of stress shared by developers, quality assurance engineers, user experience designers, engineering managers, directors, product owners, scrum masters, etc., would continue for years and one of the main causes, more often than not, was conflicting priorities.

She had gone out to lunch with Mike to chat about all the stress and fuss that folks had been sharing with her over the last few weeks. She was hoping Mike could shed some light on what was going on given that once again, they were working for the same company and Mike could share some technical details that Vita wasn't familiar with.

"Do you know what **SOA** is?" Mike asked Vita while they were on the way to lunch.

"You mean **Service-Oriented Architecture**?" Vita clarified.

Mike nodded. Vita was aware that there was a lot of tension among certain people due to the product organization having a ton of initiatives on the to-do list. But the chief architect was pushing for something called SOA, which resulted in Vita being a witness of quite a few heated discussions lately.

"I know what it stands for," replied Vita, "and I also know that Dylan is pushing really hard on the teams to embrace it, but honestly, I don't know much about it beyond that."

"It is basically a way to break up the application into self-contained components, which could be reused by other components. Think of the legacy platform. At the moment, if something goes down, pretty much the whole application is down. You know how we always talk about many dependencies among the teams? In part the fact that we have **spaghetti code** is the root cause."

"So, what's causing so much stress, then? Seems like the right direction. Plus, I imagine Dylan knows what he is talking about," Vita commented.

"The problem is that no matter which team picks up the work, they will depend on all of my teams, and as it is, they are way overworked. We just have no capacity at the moment," Mike said.

"How urgent is it?" Vita wanted to understand as much as possible what all the hassle was about. Partially, because the more she understood, the better support she could provide as an agile coach, and partially because she just missed the hands-on engineering work. She truly enjoyed her days when a developer or an architect just needed to talk to someone and would dive into the technical details because they knew she was a developer and not only could follow along, but she also welcomed the learning. It allowed her to stay on top of new technology and take a break from what seemed like a never-ending conflict resolution, which made her often feel more like a psychotherapist rather than an agile coach.

"Dylan says it is urgent. I don't know if it really is or he just likes to tell everyone what to do and get everything his way, but my job is to protect my teams from burn out." Mike paused for a few seconds and then continued. "With that said, however, there is another huge benefit to the microservices."

"Are **microservices** the same as SOA?" Vita interrupted, trying to keep up.

"Great question!" Mike said. "Honestly, I am not sure exactly what the difference is since I have often heard them used interchangeably. I know they both involve cloud environments; sometimes hybrid and are used for agile application development, as well as deployment. Both scale, which is the biggest reason for Dylan to push it. He and Gary anticipate a much bigger usage of our platform come September and moving to micro services is the only way to meet the operational demands of big data."

Mike paused again and Vita stayed quiet, hoping that Mike was just gathering his thoughts and would continue to share more information on the SOA and microservices.

"The main idea is, they both take very complex applications and break them into small components that are flexible and easier to work with. Basically, every service has its own responsibility with specific input and output, so if something goes down and one service fails, the rest of the application continues to function."

After Vita was pretty sure Mike shared all the information he wanted to share and they needed to wrap up their lunch to make it back to the office, Vita said, "I imagine since Gary is the CTO after all and he and Dylan both think this is the right approach and urgent, perhaps they have visibility into something you and I don't. Anyway, I didn't expect our lunch to be so educational, but this was great, thank you so much! I feel like I am starting to understand the dilemma. I've got no solution for you my friend, but if Dylan or Gary come around to talk about this, I feel like I know enough to have an intelligent conversation."

"Thank you for letting me dump all of this on you," said Mike with a smile. "Always great to talk to you!"

They paid the bill and headed back to the office.

A few years after this educational lunch, Vita was at yet another company embracing microservices. The topic has come up at every client she has had since working with Mike and it was often the same dilemma. When do we embrace it? Do we attempt to redesign the **legacy system** or leave legacy alone because it is very fragile and only embrace microservices for the new applications? Can we swap part of the legacy gradually?

Nobody argues that it is the right thing to do given how much data applications need to process these days and experienced **product managers** at this point, for the most part, understand the benefit of slowing down with feature development for the sake of more stable and scalable environments in the future. However, choosing between feature development, something that can bring value and revenue short term vs. the long-term benefit of the infrastructure work or technical debt is always a balancing act between product management and technology teams. It is important to know that **technical debt** is directly correlated to a **product return on investment (ROI)** and is part of its development. Sometimes, it is a healthy argument, more of a discussion, the outcome of which is both parties become more educated and aware. In rare cases, however, it grows into a full-blown conflict, causing a lot of unnecessary stress and a toxic environment. Not great for the culture of the organization and definitely not good for the well-being of the employees.

Mike was in fact able to clarify what was going on and once again, Vita noticed that most of the stress was caused by lack of organizational alignment and clearly set priorities!

2.2 Disagreeing with a Client

Vita clicked on the "Leave" button, leaving a video conference call, and her brain immediately went into the thinking and reflecting mode. Few things surprised her at this point in her career and yet, every once in a while, she would meet someone with such an opposing thought process or working style that it would force her to pause and think.

When it comes to differences of opinion, it can occur in the context of the company vision, how to solve a particular problem, management style, communication style, and even how to approach a transformation itself. Some companies choose a very light approach, planting seeds, selecting a few teams here and there, and experimenting with different ways of working. Other companies choose to rip off the Band-Aid, hire multiple consulting agencies to come up with a transformation vision, develop a transformation plan and have hundreds of teams, hopefully along with the executives, go through a bootcamp and hit the ground running. They will have processes, standards, and guidelines documented, as well as various maturity checklists in place, just to make sure that all is going according to plan.

As a consultant, Vita learned to not share her personal preference but instead, offer pros and cons in each of the approaches, leaving the decision to the client. Most of the time, she could get on board whichever approach was chosen and help guide executives and teams towards achieving whatever approach was selected, unless it was completely against her personal values. During this particular conference call, a potential client said,

Resolving Conflict

"What we are looking for is for someone to upskill our scrum masters, product owners, and engineering managers across the organization, but we don't want to be flexible, and we don't want to make it easy for them."

This is where Vita had to control her facial expression and ask more clarifying questions rather than say what she was really thinking: *Isn't the whole purpose of agile coaches to be flexible and help make the agile adoption as easy as possible or help folks realize the best approach by experimenting and learning from those experiments?*

Instead, she asked, "What is the thought process behind not making it easy for them and not being flexible?"

"If we accommodate too much and hold their hand too much, then they will have no incentive to embrace agile ways of working and we know embracing would help them be more successful."

"What has been done so far as far as persuading this particular set of folks?"

"We offered training, but they didn't think they needed it. They think their current processes work just fine and they don't need to collaborate with anyone outside their own business unit. We decided to just let them be and not offer any support unless they agree to be 100% agile, as we defined it at our company. When they agree, then we will help them."

"It is an interesting thought. I just completed an engagement where the approach was completely opposite. We first persuaded those who didn't think agile methodology was a fit for them to just experiment with retrospectives, so we focused on continuous learning, which is applicable to everyone. Once they saw the benefit, we suggested they experiment with daily standups and demos. Eventually, 80% of the teams fully embraced scrum and the rest thanked us and said besides retrospectives and daily standups, they won't be adopting anything else and will continue working the way they had before. To me, it felt like a huge WIN given how few of them jumped to adopt a new way of working initially."

"I tried this approach before as well, but here, we will be looking for you to take out a whip once in a while and do a bit of forcing."

Vita tried very hard to keep a poker face at this comment. After processing it a bit, Vita replied, "I am not sure I would be a great fit if this is the non-negotiable expectation. I do like to see results and I am very much outcome-driven. However, force and whip are definitely not my style. I prefer to focus on building relationships and persuading a healthy change."

"And if your approach doesn't work?"

"We are talking about change management here more than my personal approach. Once we define what exactly we want those folks to embrace and most importantly how it would help them, there is no need to force. The company sets the expectations, communicates them in a way that is consumable, and balances what is being decided top-down vs. when to include folks in the solutioning. It is important for people to understand the why behind the change they are asked to embrace. No one likes to be told what to do, and I have rarely seen much good coming out of using force."

"Would you agree though, that some things should be decided top-down?"

"Absolutely. The vision for the company must be set by the executives. When communicating the ask for any change, it should be linked to that vision, showing how the change will help achieve that vision, asking folks to be open and showing that there is also support in place for them."

That conference call lasted for over an hour. Vita left the call knowing the engagement would give her a run for her money, but at the same time, be the kind of challenge that brings the most satisfaction when completed successfully.

Resolving Conflict

She continued to process this concept of not being flexible in order to persuade folks to embrace something fully and wondered if at times, she was perhaps too flexible, which at the end, wasn't as beneficial to teams as she thought. She made a mental note to pay attention to her preferred way of being too accommodating. Perhaps there are other approaches, and she should continue to learn and be open to other ways of doing things. With that said, she also made a note that you should never blindly agree to what you are told or asked to do if it goes against your beliefs. If you know in your gut that what someone is asking you to do isn't right, question it, even if the ask comes from someone who pays your salary or sits high up in the organization. That, in itself, might be a great learning opportunity!

2.3 Preventing Conflict

Five years after resigning from the company where Vita's leadership journey had begun, she found herself once again observing one of those moments that was a perfect coaching moment for a leader.

"This was brave, Vita. Kudos to you for taking a calculated risk that resulted in the meeting we just had and all the improvements that will come from this. Thanks!"

Vita read the email and replied right away with the following message, "I was 99% sure it would result in something good and 1% that my login wouldn't work the next day. It was worth it."

Shortly after, a response came in which read, "Vita, you have that gift of always approaching things from a multifaceted lens and I truly admire you for your candid and valid points provided."

Vita thought again about the email she sent earlier to the high-level executive with her honest feedback. It could have potentially resulted in her losing her job, but instead took a much different turn. It resulted in that same executive calling a meeting to get to know a few coaches who were supporting his organization. Vita had been at this engagement for two months and besides hearing that everyone is terrified of this executive, she didn't know the guy at all. There was one meeting, where she was supposed to introduce herself to this executive but instead, listened to him expressing his concerns with the transformation that was taking place. Then there was a very memorable meeting a few days prior where this executive behaved in a way many would find not appropriate for a leader. On three occasions during that one hour, he expressed very loudly, "I am NOT trying to be an ASS, but PLEASE someone explain to me the objective of this meeting?"

You don't have to try... You ARE being an ass, Vita thought to herself during the meeting but was wise enough to stay quiet. This was not an appropriate thought for a coach who is not supposed to judge, but hey, everyone is a human.

Later that day, after leaving meeting attendees with a horrible taste in their mouths, the executive sent an email apologizing for his outburst of emotions. It was this email that prompted Vita to send back a detailed list of her observations and a bit of feedback. She knew they didn't have a relationship, they never even met him face-to-face, but she justified it because she was doing it for his own good and for the good of the people who worked for him. It wasn't shocking when he replied thanking her for the feedback. It wasn't shocking that her colleagues appreciated her bravery. Yet, it left Vita still doubtful that she did the right thing. In his second reply, he brushed off some of the feedback and said they would have to agree to disagree.

The important lesson of what Vita may have done differently became obvious only after Vita asked her former colleague, now an executive coach, to walk her through the scenario and answer a particular set of questions.

Vita reached out to Olivia to get her perspective.

Once they got on Zoom and were done catching up, Vita dove right in, "I had somewhat of a conflict with a very high-level executive, and I would love to know if there was another way I could have handled the situation. I already handled it, but I want to learn how I could have handled it better."

Olivia replied professionally, "Okay. So, you're looking at it in an introspective way, what can you learn from the situation. For this exercise, I will be using what is called active inquiry. It consists of open-ended questions with the hope for your thought process to expand so you can have those aha moments and reach a level of understanding you didn't have before. It would not be me giving you advice unless it's appropriate and where appropriate. We can share thoughts, but mostly it will be your reflection that can help you to see the picture in the way you want to see it. How does that sound?"

"Sounds good! Let's give it a shot," Vita replied, knowing that at any moment if open-ended questions don't lead to any major aha moment, she could ask Olivia to switch hats from coach to mentor and just tell Vita like it is.

"You mentioned that you had this conflict and you're questioning if you could have handled it better. Can you tell me what makes you think that you could have handled it differently?"

"I keep replaying it in my head, debating if I did the right thing. Rarely do I have this amount of doubt. I gave this executive feedback as soon as feedback had to be given, and the outcome of my feedback was actually ok. However, at the end of the day, I don't think I accomplished what I hoped to accomplish."

"What makes you think that?"

"I think I have to share the whole story with you in order for us to actually get somewhere because if I speak in general terms, we will not dive into the meat of the situation."

Vita proceeded to relay the whole story to her friend and coach.

"Ok, I will deviate from the open-ended questions and ask a yes or no question. Do you feel that you came into the meeting sufficiently prepared in terms of controlling the dynamic of the meeting, knowing his personality, and knowing that you know how to end a meeting successfully?"

Resolving Conflict

"This wasn't my meeting though. As I am thinking now, what I could have done is maybe coached the person facilitating the meeting so she would have started off in a different way and not given him the opportunity to blow up. I was not facilitating; I was an observer."

"Let's pause the coaching for a moment," said Olivia with a smile and then asked with a smirk because she knew Vita was about to have an aha moment. "Do we know people similar in personality to this executive? Is there a certain prototype of a person that we are familiar with and is there a better way, in general, to handle meetings with that kind of personality?"

"Ah! I know! I know! If we were to prepare him and meet with him ahead of time, show him the objective and show him the deck and ask him for help by just being there and listening to what other people have to say. Maybe if we prepped him, it would not have put him in a position where he actually looked bad in front of all of his direct reports and coaches."

"You mentioned prepping him, not putting him in front of the audience, especially his direct reports, giving him the time to process and possibly raise his concerns in more of a private setting, so he could get his buy-in before the bigger audience. If he's not supportive, understand the disconnect and address it in the private setting. The way he behaved was triggered, right? Now we see there was no other way for him to behave, given his personality."

"The situation for sure could have been handled differently, so I wouldn't even be in the position to give him feedback. We kind of put him on the spot, I suppose."

"Your initial concern was you chose to give him feedback, and then you were still disappointed with the outcome of the situation when he agreed to disagree and brushed it off. If we look back with a critical eye again, on the situation, what do you think now? What do you want us to focus on now? Is it really the fact that you chose to give him feedback and he did not fully agree that his behavior wasn't justified, or is there more to it?"

"I think acknowledging what his personality is and thinking through how we could have avoided that situation altogether was extremely helpful. That's an aha moment. The fact that he agreed with some feedback and brushed off the other, I guess is perfectly okay. He has the right to do that. He has the right to disagree with me, my opinion, and my feedback. My observation doesn't have to be aligned with how he thinks."

"How much of unsolicited feedback is generally accepted by people?" Olivia asked.

"Not much. You are right. It's a dilemma that I often have. I understand that if the person doesn't ask for feedback, it's better not to give feedback because it might not be received well. On the other hand, it's always out of good intention, out of the goodness of my heart. I really want to help this person to be the best leader he can be. If I'm coaching someone and for three months, all I hear from everyone, all this pain, and suffering and all roads lead to this one particular executive, I always look for an approach to help the situation. I was not hired to be this person's executive coach. He hired me as a team coach, as a program level coach, whatever that may be, but not for him. I understand it's not my place, but it is hard to sit back and focus on the team and the program when you know there is a bigger pain point that needs to be solved."

"Let me probe a little bit more, let me challenge you there. I see he was part of the problem and you needed to find a way to sort of unlock how he can be less of a challenge for the success of the team. If direct feedback is not an option because you haven't been invited by him to get this feedback, what else could you have done? How else could you have built a rapport with him?"

"I actually thought about that as well. I eventually partnered with HR in the context of a proposal for a leadership summit. I wanted to see what type of training they offered and if they hire executive coaches for leaders. It turned out that they do, and they had something similar to what I had in mind, a leadership summit scheduled with a slightly different agenda from what I was proposing, but they took the notes I had given and said they would include it on the agenda for the leadership training. It got to the point where I felt like I did make some progress, not myself, but through a different channel. I knew I had to let go at that point and whatever could happen or not happen next was out of my hands."

Vita and Olivia wrapped up the call and Vita realized how helpful it was to have her as a sounding board. It was not even that Olivia said something Vita didn't know before. It is just that we often get so focused on one small area, it is hard for us to step back and look at the overall picture. We might be focusing on one thing but that's not even the right thing to focus on. We sometimes try to solve a symptom instead of focusing on the cause of pain in the first place. In this case, Vita was focusing on whether or not she should have given the executive feedback, where in reality, the focus should have been on how that situation could have been prevented in the first place. This coaching/mentoring session was a tremendous growth opportunity for Vita. She was able to see what she could have done differently, and it is the learning moments like this one that stay with us and help us make better decisions in the future.

2.4 Disagreeing with Higher-Ups

Vita woke to silence but felt like the house was shaking. It took her a moment to realize that it wasn't the house, it was her. It felt like she was ready to jump out of her own body. Her heart was pounding, she had never felt a sensation like this before. It didn't feel good at all.

The day started as ordinary as any. In the office by 7am. Halfway through the day, a high-level executive, who later on became a friend and one of the people she admired as a leader and a friend for years to come, came over for a quick chat.

"Vita, any chance you are available tonight for dinner? Our CEO is visiting and would love to take a few key contributors out. I thought it would be fun if you joined."

Vita thought, *Crap, am I going to have the energy? Am I dressed properly? Should I try to get out of it? Is it good for my career to go? What career? Do I care? What about kids? Will they be pissed if I am not home to say goodnight? I have to tell my husband I won't be home...no, I have to ask my husband if he doesn't mind...* The list went on.

However, what she said out loud was, "Sure, let me make arrangements to have the kids picked up and I would love to. What time is dinner?" She knew the CEO wouldn't go for the early bird but wanted to at least have an idea when she would be home.

"I doubt he will be ready before 6pm, is that ok with you? It's ok if you cannot."

Resolving Conflict

"Oh, no problem," she replied. "I will be there! Thank you for inviting me!"

Given that Vita got up at 5am to get ready and drive into the office, by 5pm she was starting to get a bit tired and worried how she would be able to drive home after dinner. Her energy level was dropping by the minute. She went outside to get fresh air and bought herself a red bull energy drink that supposedly "gives you wings."

Well, not sure about the wings but it did give Vita enough energy for a late 8pm dinner and a drive home around 10:30pm. Instead of the wings, however, it gave her a caffeine overdose with a rapid heart rate and trouble sleeping that night. Although, it is possible that the trouble sleeping was also caused by all the excitement from the dinner. Not only did she find herself having dinner at The Palm, an expensive and extremely fancy steakhouse in Boston, but the dinner was with a CEO of an 8K people company. The CEO himself seemed like an ordinary guy. He didn't come across as someone with a very high ego who thought he was the center of the universe. They had a lovely chat. Then, according to Vita's analysis after the fact and perhaps just in her imagination, CEO ran an experiment.

"Hey, guys, look, there is someone who looks exactly like Ted Danson!" exclaimed the CEO.

"Yes!"
"Wow, yes!"
"Exactly like him!"

Vita's dinner companions one after the other glanced over at whoever the CEO was pointing to with his gaze, agreeing with him.

"I am sorry, who is Ted Danson?" Vita asked

"He is the guy who played Sam in Cheers," the CEO clarified.

Vita didn't notice any judgment in his voice having to explain to her this simple fact.

"Oh, I know Sam from Cheers, love that show!" Vita was happy to share. "Who did you say looks like him?"

"See that guy talking to the hostess right now?" the CEO clarified again.

Vita looked and found absolutely no resemblance between the guy talking to the hostess and the famous Sam from Cheers.

"Common guys, he looks nothing like him!" she protested.

They moved on from the topic, but Vita thought she noticed a smirk on the CEO's face. She wondered if it was a trick he used at dinners to see who would stand up to him, even in an insignificant scenario such as this one. Vita despised ass-kissing. Whenever she observed that behavior, she always wondered, *don't you realize that it is obvious? What are you trying to get out of it? Do you seriously think that the executive doesn't see it? They are people just like you!*

Vita would later realize that unfortunately, there are plenty of Leaders who prefer to surround themselves with "Yes, sir" people because, for some, it is easier than surrounding themselves with people who disagree and bring different views to the table, which would actually yield better results. Executive coaching would become part of Vita's job years later and it was moments like this that led her on that career path.

Giving honest feedback to **C-level executives** in order to help them be better leaders became a passion of Vita's. One thing became very clear to her, C-level executives are regular people and appreciate the honest feedback. Well, more often than not, there are exceptions. Not once in her career had Vita gotten fired for honest feedback or a healthy disagreement. Even on occasion, when the disagreement could be perceived as somewhat of a conflict, both parties involved learned something and grew from it. When asked later if there was one particular instance where she was afraid, because she could have gotten fired, she replied, "I was 99% sure something good would come out of it, so it was worth taking the risk."

2.5 Having Different Perspective

One of Vita's colleagues reached out to her fuming one day. After a few breathing exercises and jokes, they dove into a discussion on people who just tend to disagree with anything you have to say, which was apparently what caused Vita's colleague to reach out.

"Have you ever met someone who just disagrees with pretty much anything you have to say?" the colleague asked.

"Yes! What an annoying personality trait!"

"How do you coach someone like that?"

"I am trying to remember if I have had the honor. I do remember researching this topic. I think in my case, thankfully, I parted ways with the person before anything escalated. I Googled just now and got some interesting answers! Someone named Raymond Jennings answered it on Quora as follows,"

> "Usually when someone incessantly disagrees or argues with you no matter what you say, it isn't because they have an issue with what you're saying.
>
> Rather, it's because they have a personal and negative bias towards you and what they really disagree with is the fact that you're the one saying it.
>
> In other words, it is you, and not your position or opinion, that they oppose, so everything you advocate is automatically tainted in their view simply because you're the one whose mouth it came

out of, and therefore anything you say is automatically wrong just because you're the one who said it.

If someone hates you, they're probably going to disagree with you no matter what you say, because their objective is to oppose you on a personal level, and not make their own point.

Once you realize this, the next step to dealing with it depends on the social dynamics and politics, but it always begins by realizing that the problem is social and not logical."

"Well, that's kind of sad, knowing that the issue isn't them per se but the fact that they dislike you, and it could be you!"

This last statement caused a chuckle.

"Oh, there is another good answer, by someone named Sera Ha,"

If someone disagrees with everyone without rhyme or reason, it means…

1. *They've either got an issue with you (you'll know if they're just doing this with you), or*

2. *They have deep fundamental problems that they need to resolve.*

Either way, it's going to take a lot of discussions and a heck of a lot more patience and prudence. If you really care to or must continue to talk to them, then you'll want to help them resolve either of the two issues that are at play. You will need to step out of yourself and try to understand where they're coming from. Whatever you choose to say or do with them, bear these things in mind. It will be a lot of work.

Otherwise, sure, you could dismiss their dissatisfaction entirely and be snarky about it, but it most likely won't bring about any significant changes in them, and if anything, it'll likely deepen whatever scars they have.

"I suppose that's good advice right there. Speak less, listen more, and try to understand what is causing them to disagree."

As the discussion went on for a bit longer, Vita thought of a few scenarios in her career when folks acted this way. She realized that in some cases it may have been a personal dislike but in many cases, it was just a matter of a different perspective!

In one particular scenario, where it couldn't have been a personal dislike because Vita had never met the person, she got into a very passionate discussion online on the following topic,

"Does one need a computer science degree to be successful in the high-tech world these days?"

Vita shared that a degree in computer science wouldn't hurt, especially because she personally hasn't met a single VP of engineering or a CTO without at least a bachelor's degree. A person immediately disagreed with her, saying that he knows plenty of people who are very successful without a degree, and it is a waste of money. That passionate discussion included at least a few back-and-forth exchanges before Vita looked this guy up on LinkedIn to see his background. Sure enough, he turned out to be a principal software engineer and an architect who seemed to be doing very well and worked in some big-name companies, while not having a formal education in computer science. He must have been one of those brilliant people to whom writing code came naturally and with his brilliant brain and experience, he achieved what he considered a successful career. Vita, on the other hand, knew that her personal career achievements were in fact due to her Computer Science degree and there was no way she would have gotten where she was without that education. The respect that she saw when people learned she had a Master's Degree in Computer Science has never gone unnoticed and although she didn't disagree that there are many brilliant people who achieved a lot without any formal education, she wanted to make a point that education does help in achieving certain levels of success.

Once again, it all came down to defining what success in the high-tech world was. Could you be an effective developer without a degree? Absolutely! Could you be a CTO without a degree? Possibly, but the majority of CTOs Vita knew did have degrees. If a company were down to two candidates and one didn't have a degree and another had a master's degree from an Ivy League school, who would have a better shot at landing the job? Are there companies that don't look at education? Yes! Are there more companies where without at least a bachelor's degree your resume wouldn't even hit the desk of the internal recruiter? Absolutely!

Vita concluded that both she and the gentleman were right to some extent, and it made a ton of sense what caused them to have such a different perspective on the topic. Their definition of the highest achievement and success was different. When we speak about something in general terms and don't define what it is we are actually discussing, we are prone to make assumptions that lead to disagreements and misalignment even on the topic you disagree about!

2.6 Acting as a Servant Leader: "How Can I Help?"

"What is the escalation path in this company?" Marie asked.

"What do you mean?" Vita was confused.

"So, we have a situation. The team lead is super 'command and control'; he continues to give out tasks to team members. When I attempt to coach, he seems receptive but then just goes right back into his old ways and I am not sure what to do next," Marie said with a visible frustration in her voice.

"I know, Marie. I totally understand your frustration. I have chatted with my boss briefly about this situation but for now, they are choosing to leave it as is until this release is done. It is too risky to do anything. Is he bullying the team in any way?" Vita tried to assess how bad things were. She had already spoken to her boss about this, and HR was aware of the certain undesired behaviors this team lead had, but they asked to do their best to keep the situation under control for the time being. Now Vita had to somehow persuade this agile coach she had just hired to keep coaching and not stir the pot even more.

"He doesn't necessarily bully the team or anything. He just nods whenever I have a conversation with him and try to encourage him to trust the team but then he turns around and instead of empowering them and letting them choose stories from the top of the backlog, he assigns stories to them."

Resolving Conflict

Marie was getting seriously angry; you could almost see steam coming out of her ears.

"Listen, Marie, we as coaches cannot add oil to the fire. We need to find a way to deescalate the situation rather than add to it. At the moment, I don't have another team to move you to. It has only been a month since you joined, and you were the last person I hired. Could you, try, please, to just chill," Vita used one of her favorite expressions, but later learned it wasn't the best way to handle the situation. It had made Marie angry even more than she already was and she went straight to Vita's boss.

"Vita!" said her boss. "Listen, knowing you, I am sure there is more to the story, but Marie came to my office yesterday pretty upset."

Vita rolled her eyes, knowing that it is not the best way to react to someone's frustration (even if it was over the phone and no one could see her), but she just couldn't help it.

"I know, she was very upset, and I probably added fuel to the fire by asking her to chill. I understand she needs help, and she did the right thing to escalate. It is just that I asked her politely on a few occasions to hold off and be patient. I thought with her experience, she would understand. I am starting to doubt this hiring decision," Vita confessed.

"What can I do to help?" the boss asked.

Vita appreciated the offer and replied, "Marie is a very senior coach. There is a reason I hired her. I knew that particular team would be challenging but I was hoping that with Marie's expertise and experience, she would be able to handle it. Marie is absolutely on point with everything she is observing. In fact, she even put together a proposal for a proper escalation path since she thinks it should be the next step, but I was holding off reviewing it with you, knowing how much you had on your plate. When you free up a bit, maybe we could review it together with Marie, so she doesn't feel like she is being ignored?"

"Absolutely. Let's block some time on our calendars for next week. I can't promise we will do anything about the proposal at this time, but we can certainly take a look."

"Thank you! That would be very helpful. Talk to you later!"

This company hadn't chosen a scaling framework at that time, so there were no formal escalation meetings in place. In fact, at that point in her career, Vita had only heard of a few frameworks but hadn't had any experience rolling out a model in a large company. Because of her limited experience at the time, she hadn't even fully understood what Marie was talking about in her proposal. Later on, when she would think back about this situation, she wondered what Marie could have done differently… What Vita could have done differently?

Vita hired Marie to be a team coach and was very honest about it. The company wasn't looking for any **enterprise level** changes at the moment. However, with Marie's experience, she could clearly see the gaps and wanted to help. In retrospect, a lesson that Vita learned was to know when the right time is to push and when you have to do what you were hired to do and hold off until the time is right. It could be when you've earned the trust of the leadership or the team, or in some cases, when you actually have an invitation. Having an awareness of the system and knowing when leadership needs more training and when they are not in the right headspace to consume what you have to offer is key to being able to maximize value as a coach.

As far as what Vita could have done definitely? As a **servant leader**, she should have helped Marie. She focused on her own sanity and protected her boss, knowing he was too swamped to deal with Marie's concerns, instead of shifting her priorities to focus on Marie. Instead of asking Marie, "What can I do to help? How do you propose we handle this situation?" she actually said, "Please, chill!"

Resolving Conflict

At the time, she expected Marie to understand and even doubted her hiring decision when she didn't. Years later, Vita reflected and realized that it was her own servant leadership skills that needed improvement. Marie had acted with the best intentions and passion for continuous improvement, looking at the health of the overall organization and trying to solve the cause of the pain point, rather than a symptom. Vita could have used the opportunity to learn more from Marie.

2.7 Questioning Your Own Emotional Intelligence

Does he have to prove his point on absolutely everything? Vita thought to herself as she was once again observing one of her co-workers questioning a proposed solution another co-worker just shared. *And doesn't he see that he is digging his own grave deeper and deeper and other people on the call are starting to question his expertise as a coach?"*

Vita continued to debate in her head whether she should give him feedback or not. Normally, she would go for it, but with this guy, she had tried on so many occasions with no luck. In fact, not only was she debating whether to spend any more time coaching him, since there seemed to be no use, she realized she just couldn't stand listening to him anymore. She wasn't a confrontational person and understood the fact that people have different experiences and styles of communication, but this guy was something else. She started noticing that even after a half-hour meeting with him, all of the energy was sucked out of her. She was used to self-reflection and looking within herself, so she tried her best to look at her own behavior. She did appreciate the fact that he would at least pretend to accept her feedback and he would thank her for it. He was very senior and was an expert in different frameworks, but it was his inability to listen to others and realize where he fell short that worried her. After all, he was representing the consulting company they both worked for, so it was not just about him or her.

"There is more than one way to approach this!!!" he insisted.

Resolving Conflict

"Yes, there could very well be..." Vita jumped in, "but if multiple people are saying this way has worked on many occasions, why not try it?"

It was already two minutes past the meeting end time, something else that bothered Vita. As a seasoned agile coach, you are expected to be a professional facilitator. It comes with the job. To Vita, the first rule of facilitation is starting and ending meetings on time, but this guy seemed to not pay attention to time at all! He would just keep on talking. On many occasions, Vita just waved goodbye on camera and left, already late to another meeting.

Later that day, she decided to send feedback via a Slack (Vita's favorite communication tool) message. A year prior, she would have held off until there was an opportunity to give this feedback face-to-face, but since everyone has been working remotely due to the pandemic, she got accustomed to just going for it, taking more of a risk of the feedback not being received well. She would weigh giving feedback via Slack or email against not giving it at all, but on most occasions chose to give it. She justified it because she always intended for her feedback to help. Here is a template of the message she sent:

> "Feedback for you <name> (in case it helps you in any way). It feels as if you take it personally each time, we mention <topic>. In this particular case, when <name of co-worker> said she didn't think the <event> was going very well (not as productive as we had hoped), the reaction from you came across (perception is reality) that you got upset and kind of attacked her back with your comment that she doesn't even go there. Your response was very quick and came across as if you were just stuck on whatever is on your mind and you weren't even willing to entertain the idea that maybe, perhaps, it was worth a discussion. Not the kind of discussion where you start proving why you are right. When you do that, it makes everyone just shut up and not bring it up again, which doesn't make it a very collaborative environment".

Vita was borderline angry. She was just fed up with this guy. She was all for coaching and mentoring people, but not this guy. Vita had a lot of patience, career coaching was something she loved to do, but this guy wasn't her problem. At some point, she even said to herself, *I already have two teenagers at home, I don't want to deal with this guy who definitely is going through some kind of insecurity or a bruised ego.* She was well aware that she wasn't being nice, but she just had enough.

The reply to the feedback in Slack came very quickly. It said, "Ok, thank you."

The following day, the guy messaged Vita and asked if she had a few minutes. She could sense it wouldn't be a pleasant conversation and really didn't feel like talking to him, but felt it was the right thing to do. He called her cell.

"Hi Vita," he started but quickly jumped into the meat of it, "I am starting to lose respect for you."

Vita kept silent. She knew he needed to let it all out, so she gave him the space.

"There is a lot of inconsistency in your behavior. Sometimes you are ok to shoot the shit in these meetings and sometimes you are annoyed that they have no structure. Sometimes you are totally disengaged and sometimes you just drop off, which makes me feel like you just don't care," he paused.

"Ok," Vita said, allowing him to continue.

He went on for a while, sharing how he agreed to this role, even though he has experience operating on an enterprise level, and how he feels ignored when he shares his expertise.

When he stopped talking, Vita asked if that was all. She replied, "Let me try to address all that you mentioned."

Resolving Conflict

Vita was calm. She wasn't defensive, or at least she hoped she wasn't being defensive, after all, she was teaching and preaching the importance of receiving feedback. After some time, completely drained from this conversation, she said, "I don't know why this is so difficult. I have worked with hundreds of people over the years in many companies and it shouldn't be this hard. I am not sure what we can do to make it simpler."

"Well, let's process all that we shared and see what we can learn for ourselves," the guy said. Vita could sense it took a lot of energy out of him as well.

"Sounds good. Thank you," Vita said.

She hung up and found herself so tired, she went into the kitchen, got a cup of coffee, and stared out of the window for a few minutes. She considered looking for another job, but she loved working with the rest of the team. She exhaled, loud enough for her kids to ask if she was ok and headed back to her basement office.

A few days went by. Vita kept replaying their conversation. Over the weekend, while on a nice long walk, she had time to think and concluded that there was a lot of truth in the feedback the guy gave her. She appreciated it, knowing very well that he could have chosen to spare his energy and not bother giving her feedback at all.

When she facilitated training on emotional intelligence (EQ), she put a lot of focus on self-awareness. She would talk about the importance of knowing how your actions and behaviors affect others, what message one may be sending to peers when they are on their phone during a meeting or just not paying attention, and yet, she was doing exactly that herself. She knew they were both professional enough to join the same meeting the following morning and continue their journey together for another nine months. She doubted she would want to work together with him past this engagement though, but she chose to focus on her own emotional intelligence, knowing very well that the only person she could change was herself.

2.8 Understanding Communication Styles for Effective Collaboration

There are several tools available that help you better understand yourself and those you work with. Although there are many personality tests, such as Meyer Briggs, DISCs, etc., there was one communication-style test that made a huge impact on Vita's life. It all started at a leadership offsite and since it was so impactful, Vita would often share the story at many training sessions she would facilitate in the future.

"Ok, let's continue..." said the consultant from the stage, "...there are four flip charts, one in each corner of this conference room. There are about 120 of you, so this should be fun. Those who could relate to the category of a 'driver,' please go to the front left corner; 'amiables,' please go to the back right corner; 'expressives,' back left; and 'analytical' to my right in the front, please."

It was interesting for Vita to observe how some people knew exactly where they belonged and some stood still, having a hard time deciding which corner of the conference room they should go to. She knew right away she wasn't analytical, because looking at excel spreadsheets with a ton of data never excited her. She had no patience for it, although she learned to appreciate data and metrics when someone else did all the analysis and just presented a summary. She also didn't think she was a driver because according to the high-level description they all looked at earlier, drivers preferred to "tell" people what to do rather than seek consensus and "ask" whenever possible. This preference to keep peace and in part to avoid conflict applied to the amiable social style, which did describe Vita very accurately.

Resolving Conflict

Illustration 2.8 Social Styles

Seeing people's hesitation, the consultant asked if there were any questions.

"Yes!" Vita raised her hand. She was given a microphone and she clarified. "What if you relate to some of the characteristics of one style and some from another?"

"Ah, yes, you want to pick and choose, like from a Chinese buffet," the consultant smiled. "Think of one as primary and the other secondary. For the sake of this exercise, go to the corner where most of the characteristics apply. Any other questions?"

A few more questions were answered and within five minutes everyone spread out into the four corners of the conference room. Vita, along with a small crowd of her co-workers, joined the amiables corner. There were a few people in the expressives corner, a few in the analytics and the rest, majority of the crowd, was in the drivers corner.

"Now," said the consultant. "Look across, at the opposite corner. Ever had a conflict of any sort with anyone in the corner opposite yours?"

The room erupted with laughter. Vita rarely had a conflict with anyone but when she looked at the people who stood across from the amiable corner where she was, she saw her current boss, along with a few others who she definitely had tough conversations with before. They were all in the driver corner.

"Here is what I would like you all to do next," the consultant said. "Each group will come up with three things that the group across from them does that drives them absolutely nuts. They will also come up with three things that the same group does that helps them get a job done. So, amiables, you will write about drivers. Drivers will write about amiables. Expressives will write about analytical folks and analytical about expressives. Any questions before we begin? Oh, and pick one person in each group to write it down on a flip chart and decide who will be the spokesperson."

Everyone got to work. When the time was up and people were getting ready to share, it was eye-opening for Vita. Her boss at the time often came across as someone who didn't care much about people and only cared about the delivery of things. She, on the other hand, cared so much about people and feelings, that perhaps her decision-making was at a much slower pace than the boss expected, which caused them to have heated discussions at times.

This leadership offsite, along with many others Vita was lucky to attend over the years, was extremely educational. This particular one, where she learned different social styles and the fact that one isn't better than the other, led her to pay a lot more attention to the different styles. The key was to understand your own default and be able to shift from one to the other, depending on the situation. After she experimented with running a similar type of a session with different teams, she learned just how unexplored this topic was among the engineering teams and leaders.

Resolving Conflict

She observed many conflicts over the years and noticed that a majority of their root causes, besides organizational misalignment or conflicting priorities, were due to different personalities, communication styles, different ways to consume information and a lack of understanding each other. She would eventually co-create a leadership program and include social styles exercise as the very first module.

Vita eventually came across the book, *Personality Isn't Permanent, Break Free from Self-Limiting Beliefs and Rewrite Your Story*, by Benjamin P. Hardy, which focuses on the fact that you are not doomed if you were born one way or another. None of these tests meant you couldn't learn and grow. She not only enjoyed the story and the read, but she would also end up recommending this book to anyone who would listen!

2.9 Common Causes for a Conflict in Digital Transformation

"In an agile transformation, a common cause for conflict is people not understanding their roles. People are confused about who is accountable for what. Some sample scenarios are managers still managing teams and applications vs empowering teams and product owners. Another common conflict is when the performance measurement systems are not aligned with the agile roles and responsibilities. Managers, who should now be leaders, are still incentivized by performance in the old role. In this situation, they are caught in the middle and it is detrimental to them personally."

Jennifer Clarke-Burke
Agilist | Contributing Author

"Another source of conflict is leaders not fully trusting their groups or others in the organization. It leads to some level of silo's and conflict between functional departments because the power was based on how many people reported to you. Agile transformation can change that because these leaders do not have as much direct control over what their people work on. Instead, they need to set the teams up for success and step back while they deliver. That loss of control is hard for some folks to handle."

Naomi Kent
Transformation Specialist | Contributing Author

Resolving Conflict

"Sometimes the source of conflict can be organization and departments working in silos. Each function has their own objectives and priorities defined but not necessarily aligned with the rest of the organization. Not aligning priorities will result in conflicting priorities and unnecessary pressure and conflict for people in the front line. Then it is common to see people being stretched too thin, missed deadlines, poor quality deliverables and resource churn. Some leaders will want to own most of the functions as they would believe it doesn't need its own vertical. Especially matrixed organizations. It causes a lot of conflict for such resources who seem to have two bosses who don't get along."

Asmita Dharap
Senior Manager Software Quality | Contributing Author

2.10 Exercise

Preparing for a Workshop on Conflict Resolution

1. When was the last time you were extremely stressed at work?

2. What was the cause?

3. How was the conflict resolved?

4. How could it have been prevented?

5. How would knowing your own social style help?

6. If you had a magic wand and could grant any wish, what change(s) would you make in your organization or your own personal development?

Illustration 2c. Common cause for conflict

CHAPTER 3

Achieving Organizational Alignment

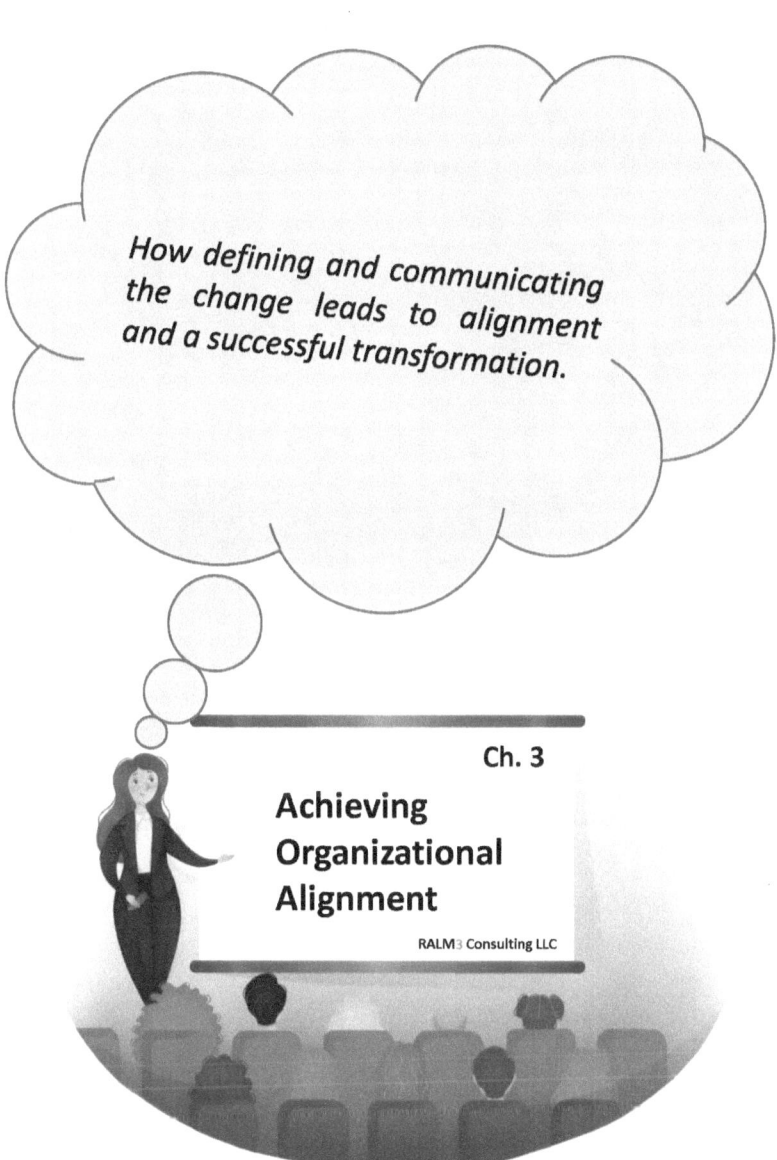

Illustration 3a. Achieving Organizational Alignment

About the Stories in this Chapter

"Digital transformation fundamentally changes how companies operate and deliver value to customers. But what does it mean for the organization internally? Arguably cultural change is more important in digital transformation than technology.

Clear vision, common goals, and priorities are imperative in achieving organizational alignment. It is not easy to develop a shared vision. Just because your vision seems obvious to you, it might not be obvious to others in the organization. Vision should concisely articulate what you want to achieve. Vision has to be able to break out into the goals that your company is trying to accomplish which in turn should be mapped to key performance indicators (KPIs) that show when you are starting to achieve your vision."

Naomi Kent
Transformation Specialist | Contributing Author

It is fascinating to reflect and realize that some concepts and terminology that seem like second nature to you now were completely new at some point. When we speak our first language, we don't think about what it took to learn it and what it might take for someone else to learn to speak and understand it. This is where patience and empathy are necessary when we try to implement any kind of change in an organization. We need to meet people where they are and understand that we might be in very different stages of our career or transformation journey.

A director of quality assurance once said to me, "You are right, teams need to have flexibility and be empowered, but they need to be empowered within guidelines and a framework chosen by the organization."

I stood there in silence not knowing how to reply. Me, in silence?! Can you believe that?

That sentence, which seems like a no-brainer now actually sounded like it was said in a foreign language less than a decade ago. It took years of conversations, discussions, debates, being in different environments, and learning how to get comfortable being uncomfortable, to get to a point where I can say with confidence that very rarely do I hear an issue I haven't heard before.

In this chapter, you will hear conversations where I heard concepts for the first time — such as setting a **vision** and having a **north star** — as well as pain points shared by the folks experiencing stress and frustration when a vision wasn't clear or aligned with the company goals and the leadership didn't know or agree on the North Star. This chapter is all about getting familiar with all of these concepts, understanding the importance of organizational alignment, and examples of how to actually achieve it!

Illustration 3b. Vision breaks into goals, which in turn maps to KPIs

3.1 Defining Organizational Change

When Vita joined an engagement where **resistance to change** was so obvious and worse than anything Vita had experienced to date, Vita called Kiera to see if she was available to talk it through with her. By this point, Vita was aware of her working style and knew that brainstorming with someone helped her organize her thoughts and come up with an action plan. She described to Keira the challenge at hand and some of the behaviors she was observing and asked for Keira's thoughts.

Keira thought for a second and said:

"Change is SCARY, but also inevitable. People often use that type of phrase to refer to themselves or society around them. It stays true for organizational change. This type of change is usually trying to address an opportunity or challenge that an organization faces. It can be either reactionary or proactive in its inception, however for the change to be sustainable, there needs to be a compelling reason for it.

In some cases, though, change just happens. It could have been a simple phrase from a CEO, not meant to change anything but affected the dynamics of a part of the organization. A common example in agile is when a VP stops by a team member's desk to make a comment about some of the work (not a team or company priority) and the person changes focus to work on the commented work without question because it came from the leader. The VP didn't mean for this person to stop working on other priority items, but the VP didn't realize that their comment was taken as an order. Do you think what the folks are resisting is something that just got dropped on them by a senior leader?"

"No, it was in fact communicated as part of the direction where the company is going. I'm not sure they actually have formal organizational change management in place though." It was only day two of her engagement, so Vita shared what she knew so far.

"Organizational change management is usually defined as an organization trying to manage the process of change by putting mandates, guardrails, and metrics around the progress of the change. The changes often spiral away from the original goals set and then it leads to people feeling like things are out of control," Keira offered another guess of what could be going on.

"In this case, I am not sure they had any original goals besides focusing on transparency and continuous learning. In the overall message, they just said the organization would transition to 'agile,' but they didn't really define what that means, which now that I think about it, could actually be the reason for resistance. The folks might not know what they are being asked to do," said Vita.

With that, Vita knew exactly what she needed to do. Next time someone mentioned that agile wouldn't work, she would ask them to define what agile meant to them. In fact, she and her colleagues decided to be proactive about it and define it in collaboration with the leadership team to make sure there was absolutely no miscommunication and that nothing was left to interpretation or imagination.

3.2 North Star, Vision, and Outcomes vs Outputs

When Vita sat down with David, a senior agile coach who recently joined her team, for an onboarding session, she found herself in that state of confusion not knowing what exactly she was being asked.

"What is the north star for this particular transformation?" David asked.

"We don't have a north star, I don't think," Vita replied, slightly unsure. She thought to herself that it was probably a great question, even though she wasn't 100% sure she fully understood what it meant.

"How do you choose what to focus on?" David asked. Another great question that Vita had no idea how to answer. She expected this onboarding session to be a very light meeting where she would share with David all she knew about the company, the teams, and the work the teams were focusing on, but instead, she was introduced to yet another new concept she hadn't heard of.

"Well, last year was all about helping teams get launched, so a request would come in and we would manage what coach would support which team."

"How would we know if we are done with the transformation?" David continued with what Vita now interpreted as a slight concern on his face.

"Is anyone ever really done with a transformation though? I thought it was a journey." Ha! Vita got excited thinking she finally got something right.

"It is a journey, but we still need to define it in a way that we know when we achieved what we set out to achieve. For example, what made you decide that you needed to hire six additional coaches?"

"Oh, because based on the company vision and the objectives, the executives decided, in collaboration with the engineering directors, that they would need to hire 200 developers. Since we had a few scrum masters that were ready to take on new teams, I thought if agile coaches would first act as scrum masters for a few months, a certain ratio would be sufficient to start with," Vita said.

"Ok, so just like the company had a vision and high-level goals, there should be a vision and objectives for the transformation itself. You would define it to support the company's vision and objectives, so there would be alignment!"

David also mentioned when defining a north star, it is best to focus on **outcomes vs outputs.**

Once again, since Vita was hearing the concept for the first time, she wasn't shy to clarify and ask what the difference was. Since Vita and David were discussing the topic of **story point estimation**, he decided to use story points to explain.

David said, "Think about the topic of story point estimation. You might say the agile organization has trained over 700 team members to estimate using story points. That's a wonderful output but so what? What was the outcome of them being trained? Are they now able to estimate more accurately and be more predictable? That would be a great outcome."

It made a lot of sense to Vita. The only thing that was still confusing was the difference between a vision and a north star. She had heard both terms used interchangeably and to clarify, she asked Keira, her long-time mentor.

"What is the difference between a north star and a vision?" Vita asked Kiera later that day.

Kiera clarified it beautifully:

"To some people, north star and vision are the same. That's important to discuss first. Being aligned as a group on the language you are going to use is critical for change to be effective. In the case where the north star and vision are used interchangeably, it may make sense to use the term vision when talking with a client.

However, when talking about the transformation it is useful to talk about them separately, especially if the organization uses vision mostly in the product or program space (as often recommended). It may muddy the language if it's not communicated properly.

Another way to discuss north star is that it is an approach to change, which allows the change leaders to meet the different parts of the organization where they are and communicate that the journey towards the north star may be different for each area."

Vita thanked Keira and continued to process it on her own. She knew most of the concepts weren't rocket science, but it still took time for them to sink in deep enough so she could articulate them in a way that others would understand as well. Vita found the best way to make sure she fully understood a concept was to try teaching it to someone else and watch their facial expression and body language to see if the information is being consumed or the person is getting lost!

3.3 Applying Change Management

"Change in an organization can become a dirty word — employees can feel like things are changing all the time, and often just for the sake of change. Anyone who's worked in a large organization for a year or two has probably experienced some level of change to org structure, processes, or tools. In many cases those changes are defined and dictated by the people running the company (C-Suite) and they work their way down through the hierarchy to the rest of the staff so by the time it reaches everyone it can become diluted or even divorced from the original vision. Applying change management methodologies can help minimize this by helping plan the effort so that communication is consistent, and that people are engaged in the process rather than left behind."

Jennifer Greve
Transformation Specialist | Contributing Author

When Vita became a consultant and began working more and more at different levels of an organization, she knew she would have to dive more into the topic of change management and apply it to large organizations. She attended a leadership offsite where change management was part of the agenda, but she hadn't had much formal experience with it. Once again, knowing that on top of her experience, Keira had studied and read many books on change management, Vita reached out to learn more.

Kiera said: "There are a lot of models for change management in the market. I try to anchor the conversation around two approaches: phased or north star change.

Achieving Organizational Alignment

Phased approach to change lays out a roadmap and moves through the phases in a managed fashion, or at least the attempt is there. This model sets out a roadmap and a plan based on defined phases of change, and then executes on that plan. This can be useful for some types of change but also may not be the right fit depending on the type of transformation happening in the organization. This approach has some drawbacks in that there is a false sense of security that everything is under control. There is also a risk that the output defined for the change becomes the focus rather than the outcomes. An example of this is when an organization runs a training (an output in the plan) rather than verifying that the training helps change the behavior or process, which was the main outcome for which they were aiming. The organization may stop asking if this training really addresses the goals or if they are doing this to check the box on a plan. We saw that with one client. They really struggled with the transformation over time because most of the people involved in the change stopped seeing the value of the plan. There was no appetite to evolve the plan to address this and the transformation became a struggle. More and more people, especially leaders, started questioning the value of the change as a whole, rather than just questioning the value of that particular training.

Another approach for change is the **north star approach.** This is also sometimes called the evolutionary model of change. There is a defined north star that every part of the organization works towards. We meet the organization where they are and move towards a common outcome. This empowers distinct areas to address their concerns without compromising the long-term vision. I coach organizations towards this model for digital or agile transformations because it doesn't create a plan that is cookie cutter. The idea with this model is based on decentralizing the change management into different areas of the company. It doesn't mean that all areas will have the same journey to get to a central north star which is the goal of the change. The potential issue for the north star model is that it can look chaotic to leadership. The approach of constant inspections and adaptive activities means that the outcome is the driving force behind the journey rather than the output from the plan, however it is harder to measure in traditional formats.

One client I worked with had two departments involved in a major change effort moving towards agile. Department A was a delivery-focused department already working in a team-based approach. Department B was more operational in nature and had just formed teams, but this was not the norm. The client started with a phased model of change, but it became a struggle because the plan worked for applying change to Department A but not Department B. Department B got very frustrated with the transformation and the rest of the organization. They were not on the same journey as Department A and that wasn't accounted for effectively in the phased plan. We pivoted to a north star model. Department B was able to figure out what was needed to get to the outcome goal and experiment how they would move towards it. This allowed both departments to arrive at the north star while allowing them to craft the appropriate journey needed to get there.

A pattern I often see in digital and agile transformations is that the higher-level leaders are not expected to lead the change or even participate in the change at all. It may be talked about initially but is never addressed effectively. They often do not realize that how they work as managers and leaders needs to model the new behaviors to help the rest of the organization adapt. This is usually called **change leadership** and is critical to the success of the transformation. When leaders do not understand, model, advocate for and problem-solve around a transformation, then their followers will likely follow suit. Leadership behavior sets the organizational culture. It is critical that this is addressed as part of the transformation efforts or the sustainability of the change will be at risk. Equipping all levels of the organization with the expectations for success with this transformation can be a powerful tool for alignment and to create an environment for change leadership to happen."

"Was change leadership an issue in the example with the two departments?" Vita asked.

"Yes, definitely. The example mentioned before with Department A and B also had a change leadership problem. The **change management office (CMO)** and the higher-level leaders were not showing change leadership. The CMO was mandating for everyone to get on board, but that behavior was in direct contradiction with the culture they were trying to introduce. Agile values a team-based approach to work, with a focus on empowerment and autonomy. Department B was disempowered and did not feel heard, and it affected their view of the transformation. It also set a perception that the CMO was an ivory tower where people had no understanding of the reality of the situation. Even with a pivot to a north star approach, the CMO still had to deal with the issue of perception and rebuild the trust by showing that they were part of the transformation as well."

3.4 Setting a Vision

"Vision is not trying to boil the ocean. Vision is about knowing where you want to go. Every organization needs to define what it is they are trying to accomplish digitally or otherwise. Clear business goals and their prioritization determines what tasks need to be accomplished and in what order. Achieving your goals one step at a time, having a bigger picture in mind and ability to think big while implementing narrowly will lead to a successful transformation."

Tatiana Thomas
Director of Customer Experience and
Digital Strategy | Contributing Author

As Vita continued her leadership journey, moving more and more into the strategic thinking arena, her conversations with Keira became more and more frequent. It was continuous learning every day for Vita, trying to navigate the unfamiliar waters of the ocean. Vita, whose default social style was amiable, would often find herself in the middle of both spectrums trying to offer help and get folks to a consensus, but finding her skill level wasn't quite there yet. In one of these learning sessions, Keira mentioned a vision exercise she had recently done.

She said: "A major organizational change is usually triggered by a perceived opportunity or challenge they are facing. This is called a **problem statement** and is frequently used to justify making a large change that can cost a lot of money, time, and make people uncomfortable, which in turn affects productivity. One of the first things I usually ask clients is "why change?" Understanding the reason can help to understand their vision for the transformation, even if it is not crafted yet.

Achieving Organizational Alignment

A vision is a tool used to help get everyone aligned. It helps with understanding value and how to make decisions to move towards goals. A transformation vision is critical to articulate how the proposed changes to the organization will address the "why change?" question."

"So, what should a vision look like?" Vita asked, intrigued by this concept.

"A good vision includes three aspects: a vision statement, a mission statement, and strategic goals. The vision statement is to set the reasons for what the organization is trying to accomplish and why it is important. This should be a compelling statement to get everyone aligned and excited about the change. The next component of a vision is to have a mission statement. Now the mission statement is a little different. It is the high-level '"how" for the change. It does not go into details but sets a direction. The final section is the strategic goals or **Objectives and Key Results (OKRs)**. This section is the acceptance criteria for a vision; the organization should be able to use the strategic goals to track progress as they move towards their vision. Overall, a vision is usually between one to five years. This is true for transformation visions as well since the company needs to account for strategy, as well as culture changes over time. **Culture changes** can take years to implement and be sustainable, therefore a vision needs to account for that too. It is also important to note that the transformation vision should align with the company vision and values. If the transformation violates the company vision or values, then the entire statement for the change should be re-evaluated or the company vision may need to be reviewed as well.

An example of a vision could be as follows:

Vision: We want to work towards business agility so we can better respond to the rapidly changing market needs.

Mission: Go through a digital transformation.

Strategic Goals:

- Company adoption of the new practices increases over time.
- Track the ability to deliver on value for the company and pivot to address the opportunities.

This vision includes the key components and is easy to understand. This statement is critical to get the whole organization on the same page for a transformation."

"Now that you have a vision, what do you do with it?" Vita continued.

"All levels of the organization need to understand why the change is happening and what the change is. Often organizations will define the mission statement but not really what they are trying to solve. That can lead to confusion and to lack of engagement in the change itself. The key part in the example above is to be able to address the rapidly changing market needs. The digital transformation in this case is the tool used to accomplish that. If this is well understood, then it can also be used as a tool for collaboration and empowerment. People at all levels are then equipped to make decisions with the vision in mind. They are all working towards that common goal.

Helping an organization to define a vision whether it is in the space of a transformation, various products, or an entire company can be done through multiple ways. I prefer using workshops with key people to align them on the direction of the organization and who should be accountable to implement the changes needed to accomplish the new vision."

"Does a vision ever change?" Vita pressed.

"A vision is meant to be a stable direction for an organization; however, change happens. The vision should be reviewed a couple of times a year to see if it is still valid. A vision should not be allowed to get so stale that it does not actually address the opportunity or problem anymore. There also may be cases where the transformation has gone on for long enough and the company is ready to stop moving in that direction. Reviewing the vision on a regular basis takes a lot of the politics out of the change because everyone continues to see the need for the change. This can also allow the change leaders to operate in any area of the organization to address any impediments faced by the transformation."

"Ok, I know I am probably pushing my luck now," Vita said with a smile, "But, after a vision is created, what other issues could happen?"

"Often organizations going through a major change can lose focus of what the change was trying to achieve. Leaders that crafted the change vision may leave, new leaders involved may have never been a part of the conversation, missing information, or have differing goals. A lot of other factors over time could lead to a loss of focus on the change. Talking to various key players can lead to completely different answers. The symptoms can be things like executing a plan rather than accomplishing the core outcome of the change and not adjusting to new information. This can also be shown through change being applied in various departments in completely different ways so that the change is not scaled effectively.

I had a client that was part way through a transformation. In this case the transformation vision statement was not effectively communicated, resulting in multiple parts of the company interpreting and defining their own view of the change and what success would look like. It became impossible to track the success of the change because it was different everywhere. This noise in understanding even though there was a vision became an impediment for the next stage of the transformation. They struggled to scale since there was not a common approach. They have since started reviewing their vision to address this critical leadership misunderstanding."

"Wow! This was definitely information overload, but so good! I think this is exactly what I need to experiment with next," Vita thanked Keira and continued to process this information for a few days.

She waited for the right moment to propose this type of exercise to the leadership she was supporting at the time, and it was received extremely well. Over the years, it would become a standard exercise Vita would facilitate for clients upon starting an engagement if they didn't have a vision in place.

3.5 Setting Priorities

"If the organization is not structured to function as an agile product development company but instead to deliver projects that take business priorities including dates as the primary driving factor, it is difficult to see proper prioritization. Tech debt continues to increase, new features and dates are initially met only to cause operational instability."

Asmita Dharap
Senior Manager Software Quality | Contributing Author

"What do you think causes so much stress?" Vita asked one of the tech leads.

"How much time do you have?" he joked.

"Uh oh," Vita said with a smile, showing she was all ears for as long as it took.

"One of the major pain points is that we have work coming our way from different directions and we are expected to somehow prioritize it ourselves. One VP of engineering tells us to do one thing, another tells us to do another and then the VP of architecture says we need to focus on something else. Everything is a priority. The messed-up part is that half of the team reports to one VP and the other half reports to the other, so no matter how we prioritize, someone will be unhappy. Our product owner, who on paper should be on the hook to do that prioritization doesn't understand the work and so he relies on me and the architect to prioritize. On top of this, he is under pressure from his boss, who is the director of product and very influential in the company. I know this isn't right and it is way above my pay grade, but it seems like I am stuck in between this mess."

The tech lead took a second to inhale some air, while Vita listened intently. "How do other companies handle this?" the tech lead asked.

"Well, I can tell you how it could be handled in a perfect world if that helps," Vita answered with empathy.

She continued: "Ideally, you would want the CTO, along with the **chief product officer (CPO)** and the CEO, to set the company goals. There should be a very clear vision of "what" the company wants to achieve and "why." It shouldn't be a very long list and the list should be prioritized. The CTO and the **chief architect** are consulted to make sure it is feasible, at least at the high level, and the high-level company goals, prioritized, are communicated to the next level of executives. Ideally, it is a safe environment for everyone to speak up, and everyone is mature enough to express any concerns they may have. Oh, and by the way, not everything has to be driven top-down. Often it is both. The C-level execs come up with goals based on their expertise and what they are exposed to, but teams also have an opportunity to bring up their ideas based on their level of expertise and what they are exposed to. Once that list is combined, ideally, consensus is achieved. If there is a difference of opinion, which is what it sounds like in your case, then someone has to make a final decision and everyone else has to stand behind it, even if they disagree. If the decision is between embracing microservices or creating a set of new features that customers are asking for, it is between the CTO and CPO to decide on the final priority. By the time the company goals are communicated to the rest of the company, there should be no disagreements on what the priorities are."

"Ha! Wouldn't that be nice?" said the tech lead. "I have never seen this done properly in our company. I was asked the other day to work with our engineering manager to set goals for our team members and when I asked if they should be based on what trickles down our way from VPs, the reply from human resources was, 'They are still struggling with it on that level, so just do your best at this point.' I mean, there was a lot of empathy in the HR's voice but honestly, it doesn't make my job easier. I am a tech lead. I like to solve technical problems. I don't ask for hand-holding, I just ask for a clear vision of what they want, and I will gladly figure out the "how."'

"If it makes it easier, we have a vision workshop two weeks from now. The agenda is to not only review the current vision and mission statements but to come up with a prioritized list of 5-10 high level initiatives to focus on for the next quarter. I also heard that all the execs were asked to read the book *Measure What Matters* by John Doerr and were discussing rolling out the practices of OKRs," Vita shared, hoping to give a little hope to the tech lead those things would be changing for the better. They also discussed the fact that if those roles are not filled, don't exist, or are not available, then the decision-making should be delegated or someone with the same level of authority should be making the decisions.

"That would be great," the tech lead replied, somewhat skeptical. There was a tone in his voice that implied 'I'll believe it when I see it,' but nevertheless, he thanked Vita for the chat and went back to his desk.

The workshop Vita mentioned went well and although there were some tense moments, the openness to discuss the difference of opinion and willingness to get behind decisions that weren't to everyone's satisfaction was plausible. Vita had run similar workshops in the past and it wasn't the tense moments that worried her. The lack of decision-making concerned her most. The environments where everyone was extremely nice, and people were afraid to hurt each other's feelings were more concerning to Vita. A good healthy discussion and even occasional conflict that eventually leads to decision-making is better than all smiles but no results.

Lack of decision-making and a desire to always achieve consensus come at a cost. She had learned that not only from hundreds of one-on-ones similar to the one with the tech lead but also seeing what happens when market opportunities are missed: talented people leave and even the most patient and talented transformation coaches give up, knowing that unless there is a clear vision and alignment at the organizational level, there is only so much they can do on the team level.

3.6 Organizational Alignment in the Context of a Digital Transformation

When Vita first became a consultant, one of the managing partners of the firm liked to say, "Backlog is the Boss!" That meant defining who the main stakeholders were for the transformation, creating the vision for the transformation, breaking it down into goals or objectives, which are then broken up into initiatives, or even further down **epics**.

We define what DONE means for each of the work items and discuss how we will measure success. There is no room for any kind of disappointment when there is an alignment to begin with and the backlog for the transformation is created in full collaboration between the client (executive team) and whoever is in a position to guide, lead and get their hands dirty at every step of the way!

See section 5.8 Measuring Success of a Digital Transformation for details on how the backlog for a transformation can be organized in a tracking tool.

3.7 Exercise

Prepare for a Workshop to Define Digital Transformation

1. WHY are we embarking on a digital transformation? What are our main drivers?

2. What will success look like? What is our end vision?

3. Define some of the major areas of change and high-level goals for each.

4. Zeroing into each high-level goal, how will we measure its progress? What are the actions we will take to move it forward?

5. What are the main risk factors to the transformation?

6. How can we mitigate them?

Achieving Organizational Alignment

Illustration 3c. Achieving organization alignment leads to a successful transformation

CHAPTER 4

Leveraging Resistance

Illustration 4a. Leveraging Resistance

About the Stories in this Chapter

"People sometimes talk about 'resistance to change.' This happens when a change has been defined and communicated but it can feel to leaders and managers that people just aren't listening or moving forward.

I find that people 'resist' change for a lot of different reasons. In organizations, leaders often define the vision for a transformation and then leave it to middle and front-line management to implement. Those leaders start adapting to the change through the decision-making process and expect their staff to come on board quickly, but they have to remember that each level has to have a chance to think through how to enact or implement it themselves.

Paraphrasing Tony Robbin's quote, "People change voluntarily when it becomes more uncomfortable to stay the same."

Engage the people doing the work in defining the change — they're more likely to support the effort if they help define it and feel like they have agency.

It would be great if more leaders spelled out how they have to change personally and shared that as part of their communication plan. People need to trust the people they're following so they need to know they're all "in the boat" together. If a leader says, "Hey, I get this is hard. I'm going to have to stop doing these things so I can start doing these to support the new direction." That can send a powerful message to staff who may be feeling like the change is being done to them and not with them."

Jennifer Greve
Transformation Specialist | Contributing Author

Illustration 4b. Importance of building strong connections

4.1 Defining the "Thing that Doesn't Work"

As a consultant, what Vita did day to day varied based on the engagement, but her most favorite thing to do was facilitating workshops. The ones where attendees joined willingly were the most joyful but once in a while, she would have to facilitate the type of training session where the leadership made it mandatory and attendees weren't shy showing that they didn't want to be there. One time, in one of these sessions, an attendee was very obvious about the fact that he did not want to be there and it seemed he decided he would make the most of it by challenging Vita to the best of his ability. He said: "agile is great for some stuff, but it doesn't work in the world of infrastructure! I know that for a fact, as I have been in IT and specifically in infrastructure for over 30 years now!"

Since this wasn't Vita's first rodeo, without skipping a beat, Vita asked "When you say "it" doesn't work, what exactly are you talking about? Do you mind elaborating?"

"The whole breaking up large initiatives into user stories and doing scrum with two-week sprints and doing this program increment planning stuff. We can't just deliver one small user story and say there is value. If we are doing major system upgrades, then it is all or nothing. Can't break it up. We also use **ServiceNow** for all these small requests and they come when they come, no way to measure velocity or predict anything."

"Thank you for clarifying. So, now we are getting into defining what agile means in general, as well as in your organization. We all have previous experience, sometimes good and sometimes we are left traumatized with certain beliefs. Let's do a quick exercise. In the chat window, if you don't mind, please type what comes to your mind when you hear 'agile.'"

People typed their answers. The most common ones were "continuous improvement" and "transparency." Vita jumped on the opportunity to zero in on those.

"We have a lot of great answers here. Let's talk a little bit about "continuous improvement" and "transparency." What could those mean in the world of infrastructure?"

This was not a trick question, but one Vita asked on many occasions. For this engagement alone, Vita and her colleagues were on the hook to train over 700 people. Vita learned to appreciate folks challenging her. When training attendees are quiet, it often means they are disengaged and just want to get it over with, especially if the training was mandatory. When someone challenges, even if it is in front of a large audience and they come across frustrated or even borderline upset, it means they still care. It is important to leverage that passion and that resistance. There are many reasons to resist change and challenge, in this case, an assumption was made that Vita was going to push scrum framework where it didn't belong. It was assumed that because the training was called "Agile 101" and led by agile coaches, they would preach scrum. That assumption came from a previously attempted transformation that left everyone frustrated. When it was out on the table, Vita was able to address any concerns, fears, or misconceptions folks had about the direction the company was choosing. When by the end of the training, Vita and her colleagues were able to reassure folks that there are certain aspects of scrum that might not work for infrastructure and the focus should really only be on continuous improvement, meaning starting up a cadence to run retrospectives as well creating dashboards in the ServiceNow for transparency. When sample dashboards were first shown during the training, another assumption was made. Folks jumped to a conclusion that they would be forced to adopt the Jira tool and they would need to duplicate all of their tickets from ServiceNow. Because this particular team was going through the training first, Vita didn't have an example of a ServiceNow dashboard to include in the training, so she went with what they had, a Jira Dashboard, causing people to immediately go into defensive mode, explaining how Jira wouldn't work for them.

"I think we can actually create a similar view in ServiceNow," the same guy who originally pushed back now said with some enthusiasm in his voice. One of Vita's colleagues offered to work with him because he had a ton of experience with that particular tool, and they wrote it down as an action item. By the end of the training, the team had a clear vision of what they were going to do in the context of agile adoption. It wasn't something big or unachievable. The team needed to understand the why behind the change and how it could benefit them. Assumptions were all cleared up and replaced with a clear definition of the change, alignment on what was feasible, and a clear path how to get there.

A few weeks after the training, the same guy who initially challenged agile was demoing the new dashboards, talking about improvements they had been making, and overall, became the biggest cheerleader Vita and her colleagues could have hoped for. Major WIN for all!

4.2 Converting from Kicking to Cheering

That afternoon, the guy from the infrastructure team who previously challenged agile was demonstrating a dashboard in a tool called ServiceNow to show number of tickets the team was able to address and how tickets were broken up into different categories, so they were able to slice and dice data to answer all kinds of questions. They were finally transparent with the rest of the organization and their work could be celebrated. He showed so much enthusiasm behind the effort, it was contagious, and Vita couldn't help but smile. It reminded her of an email exchange she recently had with Jill, one of her colleagues. In one of the exchanges, Jill emailed Vita the following:

> *"In every organization, there is a fraction of people who are early adopters — they're always seeking new opportunities and are the first to get excited about change and look for ways to get involved. And at the other end of the spectrum, you have a group of people who are seen as the hold-outs —they're the ones who are most vocal about how the change can fail. In the middle are the majority of people and they can be influenced in either direction. But they are more likely to want to support and accept the changes if they see someone from the "hold-out" group who moves to the side supporting the change. Those people are worth their weight in gold for a change effort. "If Dave is on board with this, I should pay attention. He never supports anything." Find a way to give them a voice and they will bring more people with them than anyone at the front end of the change.*
>
> *Which brings me to the idea of different ways to approach changes. Most organizations have some kind of hierarchy where*

leaders set the strategy and vision and staff executes on it. The layers between them can vary based on size and culture. Some changes are driven down through the existing hierarchy but there's a limit to what those can accomplish. A company that is trying to fundamentally change the way they do business or even what their business is needs more than that. They need to ignite a spark through the org that acts as a catalyst to make the change happen. In this case, making use of grassroots tactics will be much more effective. Grass roots efforts not only involve people at the base level of an org, but they're also often driven by them.

If you approach your change in a way that takes all of this into account, you'll likely avoid a lot of the conflict and resistance that can arise if you neglect it."

There was so much truth in what Jill said, especially when she mentioned how others are more likely to pay attention to change if someone who resisted it all of a sudden supports it. Vita recalled another time in her career when they would invite those who resisted most to the group of change agents, asking them common concerns so they could help address them. In the process, because they brought these people along, they became their biggest cheerleaders. So, inviting someone who is resisting change to collaborate with you allows you to leverage resistance on a different level when they become change agents and influencers themselves.

4.3 Building Relationships and Trust

Vita, being the type of person who by default had a ton of empathy towards people, would often share her thoughts on how nobody owes you trust on day one. Someone may appear like they are resisting change, but it could actually be quite justifiable. For anyone to accept your help or listen to what you have to say, they need to know that you are credible. Early in her career, in order to gain trust and build relationships, Vita took a trip all the way to Bangalore, India.

"Nice to meet you in person! How was your flight? When did you get in?" asked Varun, a project lead who was leading process improvement changes in the Bangalore office and had all scrum masters report to him.

Varun was one of the few people Vita communicated with prior to her trip. He was very welcoming and took it upon himself to schedule the first few introduction meetings. That first day was a blur for Vita and by 6pm, when the US woke up and most meetings took place, the jet leg was unbearable, and she could hardly keep her eyes open. Thankfully, most of the first introductions took place as soon as she got into the office, while she could still function.

"Sadna, this is Vita from the US," Varun introduced Vita to one of the scrum masters.

"Nice to meet you, Sadna," Vita extended her hand to Sadna, checking previously if it didn't violate any cultural norms.

"Same here," Sadna replied. "I scheduled a meet and greet with you and the rest of the Scrum masters, and they should be gathering shortly."

Leveraging Resistance

"That's great! I have been looking forward to meeting everyone," Vita replied.

"Hi," Vita smiled as people entered the conferencen room. "I am Vita."

"Hello."

"Hi."

After about 10 people entered the room, Varun thanked everyone for joining and gave the floor to Vita to introduce herself.

"Well, I am Vita. I joined this company six months prior, so I can still use the newbie card to ask dumb questions," Vita took a pass at a joke and then continued. "My background is engineering. I studied computer science, both in undergrad and graduate school. I was a hands-on developer and an automation QA engineer up until only six months ago. I was a scrum master at my last job as well and had done a bit of agile coaching too and decided to focus on this role full time. We currently have a team of two other scrum masters, but I am still in the process of hiring more people. Oh, and I am based in Boston, Massachusetts."

"How long are you here for? Do you plan to do any sightseeing?" someone asked.

"A total of 10 days is all I could get, but Keira, who joined my team a month ago, is coming tomorrow and will be staying longer. She is absolutely amazing. Very smart and has had a lot more experience than me, so hopefully, you can all learn from each other."

"You have to at least go shopping!" someone suggested.

Vita knew how interactions like these built stronger connections and accepted every offer she received, from shopping and lunches to walks and dinner invitations.

"Oh, Vita, we have a round of interviews scheduled for Saturday morning, starting at 11am," said Varun. "We wanted your and Kiera's help selecting the candidates, but we should be done by 3pm."

"Great! We are here to help, so please, use us as much as possible," replied Vita, excited by how everything was going so far.

Everyone was exceptionally nice and welcoming, so things were looking up. There was one team lead that Vita was hoping to meet in person to see if she could break the ice. He was leading a team that worked on the core of the product and wouldn't give Vita the time of the day when she tried to reach out from the US. It wasn't clear to Vita if he was truly busy or just ignored her because she was yet another person from the US who wanted something from him. He worked at the company for many years and was very knowledgeable, so his name came up in pretty much every meeting that required clarification, either about how the code worked, the process they used, or an introduction to someone who knew something that the new people from the US were trying to understand. Vita would have to wait a few days for that introduction, so she focused on meeting the scrum masters and the local management team first.

The new CTO from the US who had asked Vita to go to India sent a quick note to his counterpart in Bangalore and since hierarchy and titles play a huge role, especially in India, it gave enough leverage for Vita to meet with a VP of engineering and product who oversaw the Bangalore office. He was a nice enough guy, but Vita would only meet him twice during that trip. The first on the day she arrived and one more time when she introduced Kiera to him. Other than that, the guy couldn't care less as far as what Vita was up to during her visit. He delegated all interactions to Varun and that worked just fine for Vita and Kiera.

Sadna scheduled some time to go over their Jira project and ask a few very specific questions, but it became clear very quickly that some of the Jira setup and processes they had in the Bangalore office were far more mature than what Vita had actually ever witnessed herself. Nobody besides Varun and Sadna reached out much during the first few days. Vita tried to be proactive and scheduled as many one-on-ones as possible, but it was not her preferred way of working. She would have preferred people to reach out to her instead of feeling like she was intruding. She didn't see herself yet in a leadership role, so it didn't feel like she was bringing much value by meeting people and having conversations. It felt more to her like she was bothering people, which wasn't a great feeling at all.

Every day, Kiera and Vita would meet for breakfast and discuss the day ahead. They would come to the office around 10am, knowing that most people would show up at 11am. It was a great way to chat with those few that came a bit earlier. By 6pm, when the US woke up, Keira and Vita would join all the meetings that were going on between the US and Bangalore. They would observe certain interactions and discuss how the day had gone over a late dinner, around 9pm back at their hotel. Once Vita was back in her room around 11pm, she would catch up on emails and on some occasions join phone screening, since she was still hiring in Boston.

Vita had only a handful of days left in Bangalore before heading back to the US. Keira by this point had met everyone Vita had met and was having one-on-ones of her own. She looked very comfortable in her new role and Vita felt like the biggest goal of the trip — which was to make sure Kiera was well-received — was accomplished.

Kiera and Vita made plans with Sadna to go shopping after the interviews on Saturday and then they would visit Mysore Palace on Sunday. As far as the engineering lead who wouldn't give Vita the time of day, she didn't actually meet him until her second visit and only after Vita proved that she really was there to help. Vita did end up leveraging his resistance to work with her in conversations with other folks. When someone would ask, "How can I help you?" Vita would say with a smile, "Oh, I would love an introduction with this engineering lead," and in response, would hear a TON of stories on all the amazing work he has done, which gave Vita a lot more insight into the organization and how the teams operated.

Vita shared this story with her friend Nat one day over lunch, and Nat shared a very similar experience of traveling internationally to build relationships and gain trust:

"A few years ago, I was tasked to build a brand-new application in one of the very well-known financial companies. A very short timeline was given to setup brand-new teams. Two teams were created in the United States, that included people from other projects and those who were yet to be hired. The other two teams had to be built in India, where mostly team members were borrowed from other projects.

Given the short timeline and a brand-new product concept we decided to run this initiative using an agile approach where each team was focused on a particular feature. We had daily standups, planning sessions, retrospectives and it was easy for those who were co-located working in person in the US. However, it was much harder to handle the same approach with teams who were remote in India. Why? For a number of obvious reasons: time difference, cultural aspects, mostly electronic way of communication.

Given the circumstances, I was very driven to complete work on time. I structured my collaboration style with the offshore teams in India mostly through emails. I had one email that was running on an ongoing basis where you can go down the list and construct or maybe reconstruct the history of events, like a journal. It was a way for me to transparently see where things were and to help remove obstacles. There was no face-to-face communication and very limited telephone conversations. However, when issues became known I was able to address them fairly quickly.

Leveraging Resistance

At some point in time my manager came up to me and asked me if I would be interested to visit my teams in India. I was surprised to hear that. I asked what the business need or justification for my travel was. I was astonished to hear that my teams in India had challenges working with me. I came across to them as extremely demanding, controlling, without empathy or understanding how they work and live in India. My manager added that he was surprised himself hearing this feedback because from his interactions with me he was pleased and thought that I was personable, understanding, eager to help, accountable and responsible, etc.

A few months later, I was in India meeting with my teams having conversations, laughing, and building trust and relationships. To this day I'm still in contact with them, and with some I became friends. There are several lessons learned from this story: collaboration and communication through email with team members who you never met before, who reside in a different country, with a different culture, in a different time zone is not optimal. In order to build a high-performing team, we need to establish a common understanding, trust through empathy, and build shared experiences. All of that is impossible by using just email. We are human beings and more than 75% of how we communicate is through voice, eye contact, and body language. The lesson learned for the company I worked for at that time was to start rotating members on an ongoing basis, so people have a chance to collaborate. Also, when we are establishing a new engagement, a new initiative, with people who haven't worked together in the past it is highly important to bring them together at least for the initial 2 - 3 or maybe 4 weeks. This gives them a chance to build human connections."

Vita would often discuss the importance of face-to-face communication with her colleagues, given that for two years, Vita has virtually met hundreds of new people via six different engagements as a consultant.

Having never met most of these people in person, she's proven that building relationships and trust is 100% possible with all the tools currently available. It is not so much meeting people face-to-face as it is reaching out, turning cameras on, and having time to share major events happening in each other's lives. It is no doubt a lot easier for those who resist change to hide, not meeting you even a quarter way to build that trust, but all we can do as change agents is invite, encourage, and attempt to engage. None of us have magic wands and so if someone has no interest to engage with you, eventually, you do have to recognize you have done all you can and move on.

4.4 Being Creative in Breaking the Ice

Even for people who find connecting with others relatively easy, sometimes breaking the ice and building relationships requires a bit of creativity. Vita's first trip to India was exactly that and she nailed it! At least from her perspective she did. She will never know what people truly thought of her creative idea.

Alright, here we go, Vita thought to herself entering the building. She felt like a million bucks that morning. It was already halfway through her first trip to India, so jet lag was gone, and she was wearing the most beautiful, newly purchased, bright red sari to work.

Earlier that morning, Kiera helped her put it on. They carefully read the directions and even though they went over all of it just the day before at the shop near Mysore Palace, it took real teamwork to make it decent enough for Vita to leave her hotel room. Vita attempted to do it on her own at first but very quickly realized that agile expertise wouldn't be the only thing Vita would have to rely on Kiera for.

"Hey, Kiera," said Vita when Kiera picked up her phone.

"Good morning," Kiera replied.

"Do you mind stopping by my room when you are done getting ready? I need your help with the sari…. the directions seem clear, but when I am done, it doesn't look right," Vita admitted half laughing, half feeling like a complete moron.

"No problem," Keira laughed, "I will be right over."

After they were done, they grabbed their laptop bags and purses and headed out, feeling very proud of themselves. Little did they know that within about five minutes, their pride bubble would totally burst. Just their pride, thankfully, the sari itself was attached with so many pins, nothing could cause a wardrobe malfunction.

"Excuse me, miss," Vita turned around to see if the woman at reception was referring to her. She noticed the woman walking very fast towards her and Kiera.

"Excuse me," the woman said again, very politely with a smile. "Please follow me, I need to fix your sari." As it turned out, after all that hard work and victory, all the pins had to be taken out because it was pleated in the wrong direction.

The woman at the reception was very kind and patient. She complimented Vita on the sari and said that we were very close, most likely just trying not to hurt Vita's feelings. Vita was grateful. Who would want to show up at work not wearing it right!?

Wearing sari in general made Vita feel like a character from a Disney movie, but knowing that it was put on by someone who actually knew what they were doing made her feel confident. She was ready to conquer the mountains! Well, maybe not the mountains. She would settle for starting up a conversation with a few co-workers. She had a few good days in the office so far, but she was hoping a sari would help her break the ice even further.

The glances and smiles started in the hotel lobby and they continued through the entrance to the office building, the elevator, and finally on Vita's floor. Perhaps the glances were all in Vita's imagination and in reality, nobody cared what she wore, but there was no doubt there was now something people could use to start a conversation.

With some variations, most of the conversations that day were similar to the following:

Leveraging Resistance

"Wow, you look nice."

"Thank you."

"Where did you buy it?"

"Kiera and I went to visit Mysore Palace yesterday and the taxi driver took us to a shop nearby."

"How did you like the Palace? It is Beautiful, isn't it?"

"It was absolutely AMAZING! The most beautiful I had ever seen."

"How much did you pay for the sari?"

"WHAT? Oh no! Next time tell one of us and we will take you and make sure no cheating.... you paid way too much! But it is a beautiful sari. And it does look very nice on you."

"So, you are from the US? From Boston? What do you do? Oh, really? That's great! Can I ask you a work-related question?"

YES, Vita thought to herself. It totally worked. It didn't matter that she paid double for the sari. It was worth every penny. People talked and Vita listened. Vita didn't tend to take notes, not during informal conversation, nor during formal one-on-ones. Vita gave her undivided attention in every conversation, showing that she truly cared. Later in her career, she adopted a habit of summarizing her days or weeks, coming up with "Weekly Coaching Wisdom" to capture observations, suggesting a mindset focus for the week, and summarizing lessons learned and wins from the teams and leadership. People found it valuable and when a similar set of changes in the process or mindset was proposed for a new set of folks, Vita had something already written which was compelling and could be used as another way to ease someone's fears or clarify some unknowns. It was also leveraged to show just how much improvements were made and how they added up over time.

As far as breaking the ice and building relationships, Vita had no doubt that it was the only way to be a change agent. No need to wear a sari each time but being able to come up with creative ways to engage people is absolutely the key to success when it comes to adopting change.

4.5 Meeting People Where They Are

"Communication is always a two-way activity between a sender and a receiver. Someone says or writes something and it is consumed by one or more people. It's important for the sender of a message to consider their audience when sharing what needs to be said to ensure the greatest chance of understanding.

This is especially important when the message involves changes that have an impact on the person receiving the message. In these cases, it's easy for the person listening or reading to start thinking about questions like, "What does this mean to me?" Those questions can become blockers to them absorbing any other information that's been shared.

But even in regular, daily communication, it is important to consider the person on the receiving end. Understanding how to share the right level of detail — both for the person's role/level in the organization and their personal style — can help build strong connections and trust that can help increase success and engagement."

Jennifer Greve
Transformation Specialist | Contributing Author

"I don't understand what is so difficult here. Why are we going over this statement of work in such detail again when all we need to do is just add one more senior coach consultant to the client who will do a very similar thing to what Vita already has done but for a different group of folks?" Vita's colleague, fellow sr. lead consultant was visibly frustrated since they were now on a third call discussing this new statement of work with the sales team.

Vita didn't say anything out loud since there were six other people on the call who were not shy to jump in, but she messaged her colleague on the side reminding him that it seems straightforward to him because they had already discussed these statements of work, but the current client (as well as few folks from the sales team) hadn't and so he needed to understand that for them, it might require more time to process the information.

It was an aha moment and a reminder for Vita as well that meeting people where they are doesn't only apply in the space of transformations and change management. Patience and empathy towards people is applicable in all aspects of our lives. What is simple and straightforward to you might not be for someone else. It is good to have that awareness, especially when you become an expert in something!

4.6 Having Empathy Towards People

It was common for Vita to be asked to facilitate a **retrospective**, as someone who was an independent bystander with no bias and solid facilitation skills. Vita would always agree and welcome the opportunity because she saw a lot of value in this practice, regardless of the fact that it would often turn into a time suck and a huge pain in the you-know-where. This one time, she found herself listening to a request for about 10 minutes and still was unsure what the requester was trying to say. Normally, it would be a quick discussion around what had gone wrong, so Vita would know what questions to ask and how to lead the conversation during retrospective to get people to open up. In this case, however, there was so much random information that Vita was starting to get lost in what she was being asked.

"I am sorry," Vita interrupted politely. "What difference does it make what the team is called?" Vita attempted to lead the conversation towards how they would run the retrospective but was interrupted.

"I don't care about the process! I won't let tools get in the way!" this director, who actually reached out and asked Vita to facilitate a retrospective after a release had gone pretty bad, was now speaking very loudly with a lot of emotion in his voice. It was borderline yelling, and it did not make sense to Vita as the topic was changed mid-sentence, clearly proving that the guy had a lot going on in his brain. He continued outlining EXACTLY how he wanted Vita to facilitate the session.

"I really don't care about the process either, all I am suggesting is to gather feedback from people prior to them showing up, so that I can categorize it and be better prepared to facilitate the session. Especially since you are expected to have some answers as to what exactly caused the release to go down the way it did. Not everyone can think on their feet. It is best to allow people to think it through beforehand," Vita managed to interject as politely as she could.

What was fascinating about this interaction was that when Vita shared her experience running retrospectives, which by that point in her career was in the hundreds (if not thousands, at some point you stop counting), the director replied, "Well, I have done those too!" He sounded really pissed.

Vita knew that he was just extremely stressed out.

Why are you asking me for help then if you have done it? If you think you know best, if you don't trust me and if you feel like you need to control every single detail? Vita thought.

"Listen, I do really appreciate you helping," the guy said after what Vita assumed a self-reflection moment.

They agreed that while he scheduled the session itself, Vita would create a quick survey for him to include in the invite. She will then reply to all invitees and remind them that their feedback is required by Monday 3pm. She blocked off her calendar 3-6pm on that Monday to allow time for gathering and processing all the input she would receive. The retrospective was scheduled for 9am on Tuesday. When, on Monday, Vita sent out a reminder, this guy replied with more directions and clarification of how the session should go and what we should be focusing on. By 11:30am that Monday, someone else from this guy's team (as per his request) scheduled a preparation for retro for 12:30pm.

To Vita, facilitating these types of retros was second nature. However, she knew that for anyone who, in general, is used to being in control and has a hard time delegating, not seeing Vita in action prior could be difficult. Instead of being angry about being micromanaged, she chose empathy. She accepted the preparation session at 12:30pm and walked through what would take place and the outcomes expected.

The retrospective went very well and when two weeks later the same guy asked for Vita's help again, he didn't schedule any additional prep and allowed Vita to run the show. When we become experts and confident in ourselves, we need to remember that trust still has to be earned. We can't expect to receive it automatically from people who don't know us and haven't seen us in action. It all comes back to building relationships and earning trust in order to influence change. It also comes back to the fact that once you do build that relationship and earn that trust, someone who resisted to accept your help and expertise might just become your biggest advocate as well, which in return, will make it easier for you to influence change.

4.7 Change Fatigue

"We need to remember that often, resistance is legitimate, and people are just exhausted from constant change without any breathing room," said Vita in a brainstorming session on change management. She then moved into an exercise where she asked the leadership to review the quotes she displayed and put a check mark next to the ones they could relate to and saw as a potential pain point in their organization:

1) *"Most human beings don't like change; we are creatures of habits and want to know what happens next vs. embracing change and thus unexpected... At the same time, few of us like to innovate and therefore move us towards progress... The question companies ask themselves is how to compete in this environment where rapid technology advancement happens all the time... Step by step might be too long, all at the same time could be too much. There needs to be a balance of how much change and based on companies' vision/ mission and priorities to change."*

2) *"That's where alignment among leaders comes in handy, as well as the clear definition of the change, so nobody has to guess what is meant."*

3) *"Generally, people are afraid of the unknown, thus they try to speculate, and guess based on their past experiences. It gives them a false sense of security ... agile helps overcome ambiguity by breaking down large things into*

small ones that we can tackle immediately... like taking a very complex mathematical problem and breaking it into small components and all of a sudden we can see forest through the trees."

4) *"If there is a company vision as far as the north star, where you would like to be and it is all clearly defined, then it can be broken up into achievable components. If all of that is clearly communicated, so everyone sees the big picture of the change, but at the same time it is broken up, it may not be as scary or overwhelming."*

This was a great facilitation technique because it immediately got people thinking, processing, and discussing. What made this exercise even more impactful was Vita had led a similar session with team members and had collected feedback prior to the session. She could then show the difference between where people saw pain points and where the leadership saw pain points. When they matched, there was alignment on the cause of frustrations. When it didn't, it was a true eye-opener for the leadership team. As Vita liked to say, quoting Charles Ketterling, head of research at General Motors, "A problem well-stated is half solved."

4.8 Exercise

Prepare for a Workshop on Change Management

1. Let us define our messaging as to WHY the change is happening. Make it simple and impactful.

2. Define WHAT exactly will be changing in clear and succinct terms.

3. Now let's put together the steps involved in the change, or the HOW.

4. Who will be our biggest supporters? How can we leverage them?

5. Who will be our biggest resistors? How can we win them over?

6. How can we mitigate any fears people may have around planned changes?

7. Capture all possible communication channels we need to leverage. Different people consume information differently and we need to use every channel and format possible.

8. Decide on communication cadence for each channel and format. Remember that people start hearing your message only after you get tired of saying it.

9. Create an action plan.

Illustration 4c. Recognizing that inviting, encouraging and engaging is all you can do

CHAPTER 5

Measuring What Matters

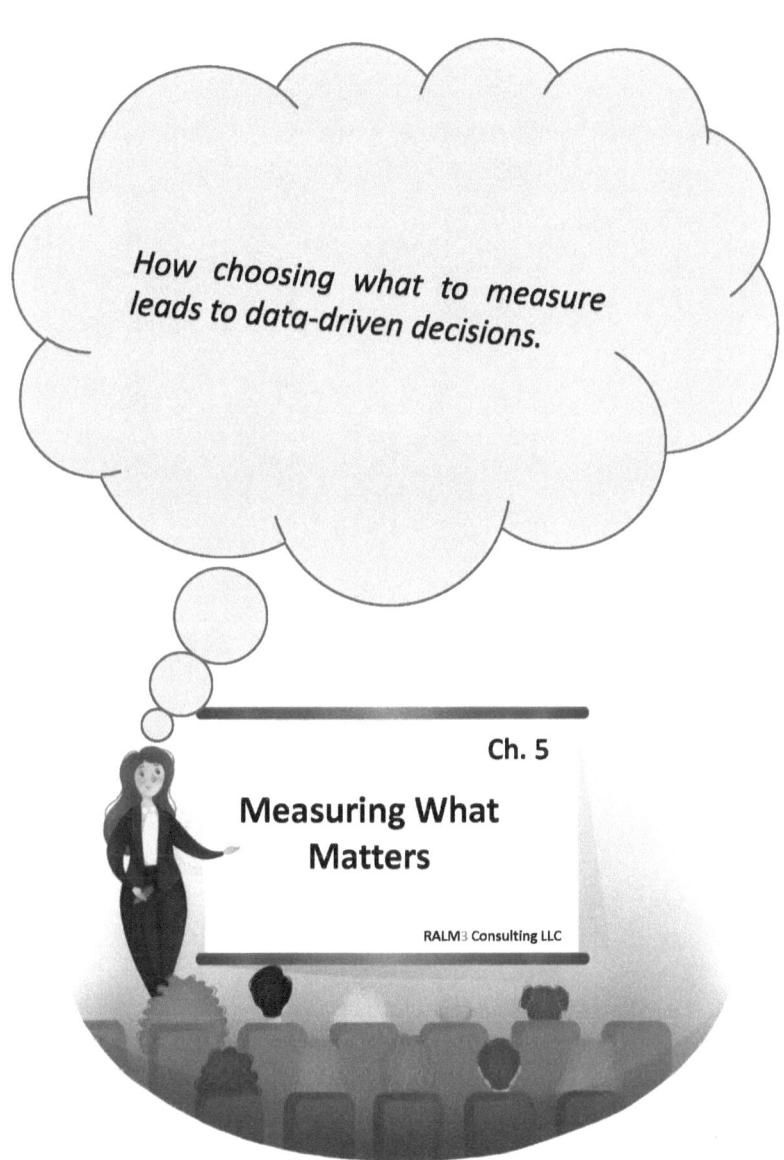

Illustration 5a. Measuring What Matters

About the Stories in this Chapter

"Healthy culture and structured goal setting are interdependent."
—JOHN DOERR, MEASURE WHAT MATTERS

Truth to be told, this whole chapter, along with the actual chapter title, was inspired by a book I read a few years ago, called *Measure What Matters* by John Doerr, so I am giving full credit where credit is due!

In Section 6.3 we will ask the question "Who is accountable for culture?" In that chapter we explore accountability. In previous chapters, we discussed conflict due to conflicting priorities, differences in opinion and even different communication styles, not to mention organizational alignment, which is key to a healthy culture. Well, setting your goals is one thing, measuring that you are actually achieving them is another!

This chapter starts by going over why we want to measure goals in the first place. We then cover different metrics, discuss the difference between KPIs and OKRs, two concepts coined by John Doerr and described in detail in his book. When I had shared with my former colleague, Sevak, that Measuring What Matters was going to be one of the chapters of my book, he not only shared his wisdom with me, but he sang praise as far as the impact of the OKRs:

"OKRs not only help with strategic alignment cross-organization but also focus on execution-based priority.

While I served as an executive coach for one of my clients, the misalignment was their biggest challenge. Each department had its understanding of organizational strategic themes; hence each developed its own goals based on that. The misalignment caused unfinished goals, loss of focus on executing, low morale of employees, and loss of trust between IT and business.

After implementing the OKR practice, the organization thrived on to the mindset of outcome vs output. Starting by setting up their key results to identify the measurable "why" emphasized their objectives to be customer-centric and align with at least one of the strategic themes.

If any dependencies between departments were highlighted in the OKRs, we made sure they were not neglected."

The passion with which Sevak was sharing how big of an advocate he was for OKRs was confirmation that this was an important topic to include in my book, emphasizing just how impactful it is for organizations to embrace the practice of setting objectives and key results. We don't stop at OKRs in this book, we just start with them!

It wouldn't be a book written by many agile coaches if we didn't include a section on **velocity** (most popular team metric in the agile world) and didn't mention **epic cycle time.** Section 5.6 is a deep dive into these concepts and will make more sense to those who are in the trenches. If it gets too geeky, just skip it! We won't know and even if we did, we promise not to take it personally.

We also touch upon the importance of measuring behavior and conclude with an example on how to measure the success of a digital transformation!

Illustration 5b. Choosing What to Measure

5.1 Why Measure?

"One accurate measurement is worth a thousand expert opinions."
—GRACE HOPPER

Grace Brewster Murray Hopper (1906-1992) was a computer pioneer and naval officer. Hopper is best known for her trailblazing contributions to computer programming, software development, and the design and implementation of programming languages.

The why behind anything, I believe, depends on who you ask and what that person values the most. Most people agree that if you don't measure, there is no way to know if you are improving and to me, that reason alone would be a sufficient "why." With that said, there are many other reasons.

Measuring allows for objectivity. In the context of this book, looking at data could break down limiting beliefs, showing you what is possible and what has been done so you see the facts rather than rely on yours or someone else's strong belief which doesn't reflect reality. When making decisions, opinions often get in the way of consensus and that's where measuring and looking at facts helps avoid unnecessary conflict and not stall on the decision making.

Measuring allows for focus and alignment. Selecting specific measurements and looking at the data enables the entire organization to focus on that outcome, that north star that you initially aligned on. Just zeroing in on what to measure will often help an organization to articulate goals clearly.

Measuring shows if there is progress. When you run any kind of experiment, whether it is in the context of a digital transformation or a medical lab, you write down results. You experiment again, you write down results and eventually, after analyzing the results, you decide if the experiment worked and based on that, decide on your next steps. This is how experiments are done. This is why we measure. As far as what exactly to measure, the next section describes in detail how to decide what truly matters.

Here is something to watch out for: Measuring does not show the context or narrative of the data. This is a key thing to consider. In organizations, there is often a fear of tracking performance that can affect how reliable and valid the data gathered is for this measurement. Understanding the story behind the data is critical to use the measurement effectively and to create an environment where measurements are not scary to the individuals or teams. The measurements should be used to track trends that in turn prompt questions and discussion. This can then lead to inspecting and adapting both the organizing for improvement and the measurement itself.

5.2 How Do You Know What Matters?

YOU COLLABORATE, DISCUSS and ALIGN!

Collaborate because this is not an individual activity.

Discuss what is possible, success factors, what is valuable, to name a few.

Align core items that are the focus for this transformation and the measurements needed.

This idea is short and simple to write but complex and time-consuming to execute in an effective way. Defining "what matters?" is critical to setting up useful and trusted metrics for the organization.

See Exercise in Section 5.9!

5.3 Velocity

When Vita became a scrum master for the first time and was introduced to the velocity metric, she found it quite fascinating. When she got to work in the Jira tool and saw how measuring velocity and having the work items estimated produced pretty cool reports, which would then be used for impactful conversations with team members and the leadership, she was like a kid in a candy shop. With that excitement, however, Vita also learned just how much frustration it can cause for team members at times. In order to measure velocity, all the work items, often called **user stories**, are estimated using a technique called relative sizing or story point estimation. Without diving into specifics, let's just say it can be slow and painful when team members have to go through every story, discuss what should be done as part of the story, and vote. They then discuss their votes and decide as a team what the final story point is.

"This is so painful," one of the more outspoken developers spoke up. "Vita, is story point estimation supposed to take this much time? We have been spending close to 30 minutes refining one user story and we have 25 to go through. How is this feasible?"

Vita had just met this team and joined their story refinement session for the first time. This question was so common that Vita seriously considered recording her voice answering it and just hitting play every time it came up. As a coach, however, she knew better. Many teams and organizations feel they are unique and although on occasion, Vita would break the news that they are not, she knew when to keep her mouth shut and just coach in the moment.

Limiting Beliefs

"What is causing you all to spend this much time on one user story?" Vita asked.

"We are not sure how we going to implement it, there are a couple of different approaches," the developer answered.

"What would you estimate it as if you went with approach one vs approach two and what are the pros and cons of each?"

"Ok, team, let's just try to estimate approach one. On a count of three, type your vote in the chat please."

"We have three twos and one three."

"Let's put this on hold for now and estimate the second approach."

"Now, we have two threes and two twos."

"Great!" Vita said. "Now if you think about it, you don't have to make all the decisions right now as far as which approach to take and how exactly you will be implementing in this user story. It is ok to estimate roughly and move on to the next story. It is good to capture what assumption you had when you estimated but it is not worth getting into **analysis paralysis**. It is also ok to be off with your estimate. There is a ton of research already done that shows how velocity averages out over three sprints or so. In general, say you underestimated this particular story, you learned from it and next time a similar type of work comes your way, you will estimate it more accurately relative to the story you had already done. I don't want to derail this refinement session more than I already had, but if you are interested, we could do a Lunch & Learn session on the topic of velocity in general, what it is used for, and some of the 'gotchas' to watch out for."

"That would actually be very helpful, thanks!"

"I will work with your scrum master to get it scheduled. In the meantime, remember, velocity means how much value your team delivers at the end of the sprint. Your goal is to roughly measure it so you can ask the right questions at the end of the sprint and focus on continuous improvement. Velocity is also very often used for forecasting, something that I believe your leadership team is interested in, so we will add that to the Lunch & Learn agenda as well. The biggest benefit of estimation using story points and relative sizing, however, is sharing knowledge and having a conversation, so it is good to spend a bit of time on it. A good practice is to put a timer for say five minutes and if you are not able to estimate a story, you move to the next one. This way you are not stuck and the product owner along with a tech lead can work on those other user stories to get them better defined prior to the next refinement meeting."

"Cool! Ok, I am setting up a timer for five minutes! Let's go!"

The team chuckled and continued with their **refinement session**. They were extremely grateful for the tips because they all felt the pain of long sessions and couldn't wait to get through it as quickly as possible. After all, what they loved doing most was actually writing code, not sitting in long painful meetings. Helping teams reduce pain and stress caused by doing things they liked to do the least was in line with Vita's mission of reducing unnecessary stress at work. It always brought her a ton of satisfaction to see improvement in the stress and pain-reducing department.

5.4 KPIs vs OKRs

It took Vita pretty much a whole decade to see how all the pieces of an organization, from company objectives to velocity, are actually connected. Being able to answer the two simple questions of what success looks like and what is in place to actually measure that success is what differentiates a successful transformation from just going through the motions.

As a junior developer, when Vita started her career, words like KPIs and OKRs didn't mean much to her. Even if she heard them in a meeting or maybe even in a one-on-one with her manager, it never really registered. Vita was given specific work and that's what she would focus on. For most of her development career, she had absolutely no idea how what she worked on fit into the larger goals of an organization. It was not because those goals weren't set or communicated, most likely they were, however, for a junior developer who was overwhelmed with the technical side, she just didn't have the mental capacity to consume all the "extra" information. Diving into KPIs and OKRs later into her career was pretty much the same as diving into velocity earlier in her career but on a larger scale!

Now that Vita has been at many engagements and has seen how different organizations and different business units within those organizations operate, more and more of her former colleagues would reach out for a quick consult. One common question that happened to be the center of the conversation in this particular catch up was the following:

"Vita, what do you typically measure besides velocity? We need to choose a few main KPIs and focus on improving those."

"What do you have currently in place on the organizational level?" Vita asked.

"Well, customer support has **service-level agreements (SLAs)** and we look at the ticket resolution times. It is linked to a larger strategic goal of customer satisfaction. We do look at a **net promoter score (NPS)** and had a goal for this year to improve that by a certain percentage, don't remember off the top of my head what exactly that was."

"What other company objectives have been set for this year?"

"Good question. I feel like I should know but I am actually not sure."

"It makes it much easier to decide on the KPIs when Objectives, along with key results are set first. For example, if we know we want to improve the NPS score and we have a clear key result, such as "we will increase the VALUE we deliver to our customers by 10 percent," we can focus on a popular and effective KPI (in the agile world) such as epic cycle time! Epic cycle time is usually defined as the time it takes from the first user story of that epic going to in-progress state to the last user story of that epic making its way to production."

"How will we measure the 10 percent increase though?"

"Ah, great question! You need to establish a **baseline**. By the way, how well defined are your epics at the moment? Are they written in a way that when completed, they actually deliver value to customers?"

"Some are and some could use improvement. Sadly, many epics are written as just a bucket containing different types of user stories and never get closed. They just linger for months and in many cases years."

"Sounds like we know what we need to focus on then," said Vita with a smile. "Perhaps you could benefit from having a working session focusing on setting the team goals based on the company goals of improving the

Limiting Beliefs

NPS score. This is how it works. It supposed to trickle down and all the teams' goals and individual goals should be connected to the higher goals set by the organization."

"It makes a lot of sense, and it is clear just how early we are in our transformation."

"It is alright...you have to start somewhere! As long as the vision is clear of where the company wants to go, you all can figure out how to get there. One step at a time!"

After Vita wrapped up this call, she thought about the fact that epic cycle times makes a ton of sense if you actually adopt an agile way of working. It happened to be her area of expertise and more and more companies were moving in that direction, but it is a very specific metric in the world of agile. Regardless, having clear objectives, as well as knowing how you will achieve them and how you will measure that you achieved them is agnostic to a methodology. The whole concept of breaking work down in chunks without losing the connection to the bigger picture and measuring what it takes to get it to completion is also agnostic to agile and is just a good practice regardless of the methodology!

5.5 Having a Baseline Across the Organization

"Vita, could you help us define goals for this next phase of our transformation, please?" Josh asked.

Josh was leading the agile transformation with a client and although this engagement didn't start with defining the baseline of the agile maturity level of the whole organization, it was now a good time to suggest defining a baseline first, before setting any kind of goals.

"I thought about it while snowshoeing up the mountain yesterday," Vita shared knowing Josh was aware by now that any outside activity was when Vita did most of her creative thinking. "Any insights that we have so far about where teams are in their agile journey is a bit scattered and we don't really have a way to see where we are as an organization. We have this tool we use, and there are others I suppose, but this one is free and simple. It is an excel spreadsheet (believe it or not), which has a list of categories such as "goals and objective," "business value," "delivery," "continuous improvement," "transparency," and so forth, along with a definition for each category of what exactly it means to be a beginner, an expert and all in between. It is usually used with the whole team, where they review each section, share where they think they are, discuss and come up with areas for improvement. It is a structured, tightly facilitated session where the final output is a collection of teams self-assessments. Because we do this as the overall organizational effort, we can report out where we are on the organizational level. For example, we can say, out of the 50 teams that went through this exercise, 30 assessed themselves as a 3 in the category of transparency. Based on these results, we can then set goals as far as where we want to get to. Does it make sense?"

"It does. In theory. Can we review this tool at some point?" Josh asked

"We can. I will show you what we have at the moment, but keep in mind, we will have to modify each section to make sure it is relevant to your environment. Even though, I am sure we will be able to leverage a ton of what is written there now, we need to make sure we go through and modify sections to make them most relevant and applicable. I can definitely show you the sample of the final output though, just so that it is clear what we would be getting after this exercise."

"Perfect! Thank you, Vita!" said Josh and wished Vita a nice weekend.

One thing Vita appreciated the most about working with Josh was the fact that he was game for anything that was suggested. Josh was the kind of a leader who wasn't afraid to ask for help, didn't need to prove to anyone he was in charge and always could articulate the outcome he was looking to achieve. Vita has done the exercise of setting a baseline for many clients now and it has always proved to be very valuable. It was not just about the final artifact which helped to set the goals for the transformation. It was those conversations during the exercise itself, which were extremely beneficial. It allowed team members to have impactful discussions, set coaching goals for themselves and learn along the way what it means to be an expert in a certain category. In some way, everything that was listed in all those different categories under the expert, the highest level of maturity, was in fact that north star. It was written in a way to show and plant seeds as far as what the "end result" could be, even if it was a long journey to get there!

5.6 Measuring Quality

"You know Asmita," said Vita, "I often think back to when I was a QA engineer. Because it just so happened that I was a developer first, I found it very difficult to understand what made some developers choose to throw their code half-baked over the wall to me, knowing that I will most likely find a ton of bugs. Not all developers. In fact, there were some that were the opposite, they were extremely thorough, almost to a fault. We are talking about taking pride in the code you write. It is really your personal brand, your reputation at stake, isn't it?"

"It is nice when people take pride in delivering useful, impactful, and quality features and products, yes," Asmita , who was a quality expert, agreed.

"How do you then go about having those tough conversations when you see the quality is just not where you want it to be? And when I say you, I really mean on the organizational level."

"It helps to have data for those types of conversation, so it doesn't come across as personal. If we have company goals and objectives and we can present data showing that we are not quite cutting it, we can discuss what we can do to get back on track."

"What do you typically measure? We can talk in general or very specific to quality."

"Sure. In general, what you choose to measure differs based on a company, industry, what sort of **software development life cycle** you follow, what **methodology** is used, but essentially think about what it means to deliver quality products. What does it mean to deliver useful, impactful, high-quality features, products or solutions?" Asmita paused for a second, but Vita remained quiet to let her continue.

> "Measurement can be at a product level, it can be uptime, it can be at a team level too, such as velocity, for example. It can also be at a feature, epic or user story level, where you measure how you track towards the completion of a feature, for example. You may choose to report on how many epics or stories are left to get done and you can also choose to report on how many new bugs have been introduced. You can measure code coverage to make sure you have regression tests to ensure you haven't broken any functionality that had been in production."

> "To improve, you definitely need to measure but you have to also be very careful and not measure way too many things."

> "Absolutely. Nothing is free if you think about it. To measure accurately, you need to have clean data in the tools. There is a cost associated with that too. Not to mention reporting on the chosen metrics as well."

> "Yes, and having clean data is also a big challenge. I have seen not just lack of standard labels or fields across teams but also each team logging defects in a different way, triaging them with different definitions for severity."

> "How about when sprint starts without all the user stories refined and then there is this catch up of user stories being written and added during the sprint, which shows up in the reports as **scope creep** and you have no idea if it was truly a scope creep or teams just not spending time upfront refining, estimating and planning properly."

> "Absolutely. It takes a certain discipline. That's when I would say if a team just starts working this way, a solid scrum master or an

agile coach, at least for the first few months is a must. Just to show the team the true value of the scrum framework and how it helps achieve agility, if that's what they have chosen for their methodology."

"I couldn't agree more, Asmita! Speaking of agile coaches and metrics, I remember having a discussion with 12 experienced coaches on what we should measure. If we wanted to focus on delivering value to the customer and delivering value as quickly as possible, we thought epic cycle time would be a great metric to focus on. We had seen a few different definitions and went with "It is from the first user story in that epic going into "in progress" state until the last story of the epic is DONE." We were trying to decide if "DONE" should mean in the production or **QA environment** and decided to hold off on production until the whole epic had been tested in the QA environment first."

"It makes a lot of sense. I have seen other companies focus on epic cycles too. If you think about it, for you to measure epic cycle time, everything has to fall into place. Data has to be clean and frankly the mindset and behavior and how you define epics and how you approach test automation. We often have to persuade all levels of the organization that we need to invest time into automation. It cannot be an afterthought."

"Spot on! Once we were able to establish a baseline, which by the way wasn't a very easy task to do, it took a large team of agile coaches about a year to implement it across the organization… we could discuss how in order for us to REDUCE EPIC CYCLE TIME, which means deliver value to customer faster, we have to work on actually defining our epics as thin vertical slices, which also requires skills, experience as well as willingness as a product owner to work with agile coaches, architects, UX designers, and delivery team members. QA cannot be an afterthought, 100% agree with you. It takes tremendous collaboration on everyone's part, but it does work, and it is worth it! Once you see it work beautifully, you can't imagine working any other way, honesty."

"So true! So, we covered a lot of general concepts now. Would you like to dive into some of the challenges when it comes to automation or talk about QA specific metrics?"

"Yes! So, I had one specific question to start with. You know how velocity is a very common metric these days? What I have seen on many occasions is you look at the velocity, sprint over sprint, and you see it increase. At first glance, you think it is all great but when you start paying a lot of attention, you notice that teams create separate tickets for bugs that they themselves introduced while working on user stories. So, it is very deceiving because it is not like they are adding more value. What is the best way to approach this situation? Do you estimate bugs found in the sprint?"

"Let's go back to what development life cycle the team has agreed to. What standards has the organization chosen to follow? Have you established best practices, so it is common across all teams? Say you agreed to log defects for stories rather than actually return those stories from being done to back in progress. Say, you made a commitment in your sprint to work on these particular five stories. Let's say one of the stories goes to QA and it seems like something doesn't work properly. You need to decide whether to log or not to log. That is a crucial point that the team needs to be on board and have an agreement about, because in my opinion, if the story goes to QA and it breaks, it's not complete. So, the work is not complete. It's not a new defect. It's just something that needs to be fixed. Whatever bandwidth you need to fix that's just in scope of that story. If you have estimated that as five story points, just fix it and make it work. Learn something from it for next time. Then we can talk about a nuance if you found something, but it is not part of the **acceptance criteria** but now we are diving into more nuances."

"Oh I know, this might be too much detail for the sake of the book but it is such an important topic which I know had caused so much confusion at some point for me, I feel like we need to get it in writing once and for all so others don't have to suffer," Vita said with a smile because she knew Asmita knew exactly how she felt.

"Seriously though," Vita continued. "One last point on this, I wanted to confirm that anything that is found in production is filed as a bug and gets estimated with points and now we need to talk about metrics that are specific to QA."

"Yes," Asmita confirmed. "Bugs found in production are filed as bugs and estimated. As far as QA metrics, we continually have conversations on how best to represent and report on quality. Different metrics are important to different audiences. The higher leadership does not care about how each card in the sprint was closed (with/without automation for example), whether we completed the sprint with some scope creep or what the **WIP limit** was for a given sprint. Some folks really care to know how many features were deployed to production, what the time to market is, as well as how long it took from feature conception to delivery."

"For the longest time we discussed and debated on what to measure, what is important to report on. In the meantime, teams were getting the work done without measuring anything. They didn't hold any retrospectives either."

"So, what was the challenge in choosing which metrics to focus on?"

"Well, challenge number one was we were looking for that "perfect one," so perhaps we faced a bit of analysis paralysis, and second, we were looking for consensus among 30 program managers."

"Ah, I see. Persuading 30 people may be a challenge for sure. Were there 30 different agile teams too?"

"You know, Vita," Asmita said, "I have actually documented once an example of an interaction with one of the program managers, which you might find interesting. I will gladly share it with you."

"I would love that! Thank you!" Vita said. A few days later, received the following from Asmita:

Proposed Metric - A Conversation with a Program Manager (PM)

> "Hey, I have put together a few slides to walk us through the proposed metrics and the way to report and trend them. The crux of which being – we want to understand the "why" behind these particular metrics, want to start with simple three metrics and make a self-served dashboard available so no one has to sit and create a report at the end of the sprint," said Niva, a QA lead.
>
>> "Hmm, these are ok, but I have all the information I need on my team, and I don't want to spend more time analyzing anything more," politely refused the PM.
>
> "Sure, is there anything in particular that you measure and where/how do you share the insights with your team?"
>
>> "Well, we have daily stand ups and I know what the status of the project is. The sprint work gets mostly done except that automation can't be completed in the same sprint and sometimes we must move the tickets to the next sprint due to bandwidth constraints."
>
> "Ok, Let's see what value the proposed metrics can add," concluded Niva and proceeded sharing the proposal but didn't go too far.

"We have a very unique situation," said the PM. "Let me explain some of our challenges with testing. Before we dive into the nitty gritty technical details, however, can we talk about who owns quality? The reason I ask is because while I appreciate your effort to figure out how best to support the team and measure the right things so we can improve, I don't even have clarity on who is accountable on the end-to-end testing."

"I feel like it is a much bigger discussion. May I just quickly walk you through the proposal so you can think it over and then we can schedule a separate meeting for the ownership topic? I might need to pull in a few other people for that one to make sure we are all aligned on that."

"That sounds good actually. I will think about who else we might want to pull into that one as well."

With that, Niva proceeded to walk thought the following 3 suggested metrics:

- **# of regressions introduced in the sprint**
- **% of tickets completed within sprint automation**
- **# of times tickets had to be reopened**

She explained what value each metric would bring to the team, the leadership team, as well as the organization. She quickly showed a Jira dashboard, knowing that this was something program managers usually found very useful. The fact that it would always be up to date, automatically, as long as the data was in the tool was a huge plus. Many of the program managers still heavily relied on status meetings and excel spreadsheets. Although they didn't think there was a pain point of any kind and they were really all set with whatever tools they currently *had, this Jira dashboard with these metrics was clearly a big upgrade.*

The conversation went back and forth and Niva was able to prove the value of measuring a select few things going forward to gain insight into what process changes would help the team. She explained to the PM that for every company, product, and team the metrics that make sense will differ, but these were the few metrics that were chosen for their organization and they were hoping to start measuring some common things that were applicable across the board.

Agile way of working may not be applicable to all readers, but this conversation shows the level of detail that agile coaches and digital transformation coaches pay attention to. It shows the day to day of what happens among development teams and the challenges they face. It shows the importance of measuring what matters for the organization as a whole, with all the bits and pieces connected. This level of detail could spark some ideas to experiment with even for those who haven't embraced agile way of working but do still want to embrace digital transformation. Answering questions such as "What does success look like?" and "How will we measure it?" helps in the journey of digital transformation, regardless of what methodology is used.

5.7 Measuring Behavior

Let's start this section with an exercise! Think of it as an ice breaker.

Which of the following speaks to you the most?

1) "It may be possible to deliver for customers while still burning out your staff. However, with worst behaviors being unleashed, it means people being pushed to the edges and that makes quality of deliverables suffer, eventually creating unhappy customers. Also means soon enough employees go silent, stop caring and start looking for a better work environment. Velocity and quality won't be sustainable. All said and done, all of us are in the people business. It's all about people, and customers can be internal or external."

2) "Doesn't everything measure behaviors? It's cause and effect. How the team behaves, if they are following agile principles with agile mindsets, the effect will be meeting goals, being predictable, etc."

3) "There is no perfection in agile, only continuous improvement and the ability to handle change. If the customer is happy today it doesn't mean they will be happy tomorrow. Their needs evolve... if teams are burned out, they make mistakes that take money to fix and cause delays so Wall Street (another form of a customer) and the end user will not be happy. In some cases, Wall Street-happy overrides customer and employee-happy and that's where the important role of a manager comes in."

> 4) *"Managers are often folks that were brilliant engineers, so they get promoted and now they are not sure what is truly required of them. People management is a completely different skill and if say their managers also focus only on delivery, then they wouldn't be the ones coaching managers to behave in any different way from the way they behave."*

Behavior is one of those things that is much harder to measure and even harder to coach. If someone reaches out and asks a coach to observe them and give immediate feedback, then there is at least a chance to help someone change their behavior. It is difficult even if the person is willing, however, if someone is aware that their behavior is undesirable and doesn't want to change, you might as well walk away. With that said, Vita was aware, based on her own experience, that walking away is extremely hard for a coach who truly cares and wants to help not only the people around the person but that person as well. Vita turned to her small group of contributing authors with the following question:

> "Hi you all! Here is a question for you! Say, we have all the epics written perfectly, they all get closed within a couple of sprints and clearly deliver value to our customers. Say, even, the NPS score that we set out to increase by X% was increased and our customers had never been more delighted. At the same time, our turnover had been higher than ever. Our employees either got burned out delivering to satisfy this goal or just left because when their management was under a lot of stress to meet these goals, the worst behaviors were out in the open causing employees to quit as soon as there was an opportunity. What do we do now? How do we measure behavior?"

One of the contributing authors challenged this scenario saying the two scenarios couldn't coexist because when you have miserable employees, it is not possible to have delighted customers. Vita, however, has seen successful deliveries but at a very high price of burnout and many people leaving. Another contributing author said there were companies that seemed to be doing well but not treating employees right. Turnover was easy to measure in dollars. You spend a ton of money recruiting, onboarding, and training. Velocity drops when team members change. You can also track employee NPS by asking questions such as "Would you refer a friend to work here?"

After a few more opinions were shared, Vita said, "I think it all comes down to the values of the organization. If they have come up with what their values are and have practices like **360 reviews** in place, then they can keep track of how many times a particular leader received constructive criticism. If they conduct exit interviews and actually do something about the feedback, then eventually people either accept coaching and work on their behavior, leave the company, or get let go. There is really no other way. Companies have to measure behavior, put support in place on all levels of the organization, and teach skills like giving and receiving feedback. I truly believe it is the only way to have a healthy organization."

Now Vita realized that she was on a roll, remembering scenarios where people would raise concerns, but nothing was done about it.

Measuring isn't enough. After all, leaders have to also be accountable for having those tough conversations when necessary and even making tough decisions. Vita had thanked the contributing authors for the great discussion and wished them a great night. There was a lot to unpack here. Now Vita's brain jumped to the topic of accountability and who is accountable for the company culture and what it means to be a leader. All of the chapters and sub-chapters in her new book "How to FYAIL in Digital Transformation" were becoming more and more connected. Measuring the right things leads to transparency, alignment, and accountability. Ability to have open healthy conversations about the metrics and what they represent and what needs to be solved for leads to healthy cultures where employees are not pulled in different directions, which does lead to happy customers and maximum value delivered. It is truly all connected and to succeed at a transformation, we do need to look at the whole picture.

Limiting Beliefs

As far as behaviors, Vita often talked about emotional intelligence and how being able to self-reflect and be self-aware is one of the most important skills to have. She went as far as offering a program as part of her RALM3 Consulting company based on her memoir, "Life Worth Living," which focused on self-reflection, vulnerability, and taking small steps towards achieving what you set your mind to, whether it is a more positive outlook on life or specific behaviors one might want to embrace.

5.8 Measuring Success of a Digital Transformation

At the start of an engagement, whether you are a consultant or a full-time employee supporting internal teams or your whole organization, if there is a list of services or deliverables, or outcomes that you are on the hook to deliver, it is good to be transparent. You lead by example and do what you expect your teams to do. Whatever way you choose to set up your projects or team's backlogs and track the progress of their work, you can track your digital transformation exactly the same way. Just like we expect teams to be transparent, define value, measure what matters, and demonstrate their progress, we need to do the same! Transformations aren't only for teams. The rules of the game are the same on all levels of the organization.

"Vita, can you please walk us through the statement of work to see how we are doing? It has been three months now and we want to make sure we are accomplishing what we committed to," asked the transformation leader at one of Vita's engagements.

"Sure, let me share the statement of work, along with our transformation Jira project, so I can show you first how all the outcomes captured in the statement of work were actually converted into epics in Jira."

> "That would be great, thanks. I love the transparency of how you are tracking it all. Many of our teams use Jira for delivering

projects this way, but we haven't thought of actually tracking our large transformation this way."

"Here is an example of how we are tracking it all. Here you see in the statement of work we were to deliver specific workshops, including a scrum master summit, product owner training and a leadership training. We also have here "coach product owners and scrum masters, partner with HR to identify incentive programs, partner with finance to review budget allocation in the world of agile, etc." All of these are now epics in Jira. In some cases, what was listed in the statement of work was really more of a high-level objectives, so in that case, we have a few epics written to account for a larger effort."

"That's awesome. So, what is currently done and how do we know if we are tracking according to the plan?"

"Each epic was written in a way that it could be closed in three months at most. Usually, we try to write epics small enough to close within a couple of sprints but for the sake of this effort, we figured it was fine to keep it under three months. Each epic has a release number associated with it, so you see each epic and each user story under that epic is marked with the month of when it will be done. Everything that was listed in the statement of work to be completed in month one, is marked with February release version. Everything that was to be completed in month two, is marked with March release…We can run Jira reports and if we look at **Jira Align Plugin**, you can actually see progress of each epic and when it will be done."

"This is great stuff! Was there anything in the last three months that came up that derailed you from this effort?"

"Everything that has come up so far is all relevant to this work. Let me show you one more thing, which is relevant in the way we track this transformation effort. Do you see these six sprints created in Jira? Everything that I knew in advance based on the statement of work was broken up into epics and user stories and actually put into the sprint where I guessed the work would happen. It was a pure guess based on my gut feeling initially. We have sprint ceremonies, just like we would for developing a solution, so we have refinement sessions, planning, demos. I refine all the user stories prior to starting the two-week sprint and if I see that something will slip, I move it to the following sprint, knowing in advance if we are overcommitting and if something needs to be reprioritized. We also have a general backlog, so if anything comes up during observation or when someone has a great idea, I capture it. At this point, I do have a release version, which is called "Later." This is something that we need to go over and see if we should plan it for the future. None of this is part of the current statement of work but we are capturing it to make sure it doesn't get lost."

"Can we take a look at what we currently have planned for the next few sprints and the general backlog?"

"Sure! You can see we closed these two epics last week; this one is targeted to be closed the following sprint. Prep for the scrum master summit is scheduled for sprint five and targeted to be delivered in sprint six. The general epic of coaching actually has user stories based on each individual coaching session, so if you were to ask who took advantage of the coaching opportunity, I could easily filter that epic and share how many coaching sessions were done. I don't share details but do track who the sessions were with and if there were major outcomes or action items that are ok to share."

Limiting Beliefs

"This was a very detailed example. Thank you. I love it. This is extremely helpful for communication on all levels of the organization as well. The way we came up with this statement of work, initially, was based on the high-level objective that was set by our CIO. We need to focus big time on **digital solutions** and our CIO is a big fan of agile, so there is a lot of focus on embracing the agile way of working. The way you track all of this effort can directly be connected to a larger objective, which is perfect! In fact, I think we need to track ALL of our agile and digital transformation efforts this way because right now, I have hundreds of sticky notes all over my wall and two large whiteboards. I am starting to lose my mind. We have so many things happening in parallel. As I was listening to you, I was thinking we need to do high-level planning for our coaching team and get it all in a Jira project, so we could be transparent, measure our transformation success and clearly see if something needs more hands-on deck in order to succeed."

"Glad you found this helpful!"

Tracking transformations this way was a practice Vita embraced way before becoming a digital transformation consultant. It came out of an important lesson Vita faced earlier in her career when she was asked what she actually had done in the last six months as an agile coach and what they had accomplished as an organization. The question came as a surprise. After all, didn't they just see? Well, no. One should never expect others to just see progress without looking at the supporting metrics. Tracking all the effort and visually representing all the small wins over many months allows you to see how continuous learning and small improvements add up to BIG IMPROVEMENT AND BIG WINS!

5.9 Exercise

Prepare for a Workshop to Define Objectives, KPIs, and Metrics Across the Organization

1. Let's look at the big picture first. Why are we embarking on a digital and/or agile transformation?

2. What will this organization look like when we have succeeded with the transformation? Let's talk about our vision.

3. Now that we have our vision, let's brainstorm what strategic goals and objectives we need to focus on in order to get there?

4. Next, let's prioritize our objectives.

5. For our top objectives, let's figure out how we are going to know that we have achieved them. What are our acceptance criteria?

6. How can we measure our progress towards the objectives? What metrics or KPIs could be helpful? Let's be discerning and only measure what really matters.

Limiting Beliefs

Illustration 5c. Importance of choosing what to measure

CHAPTER 6

Mastering Accountability

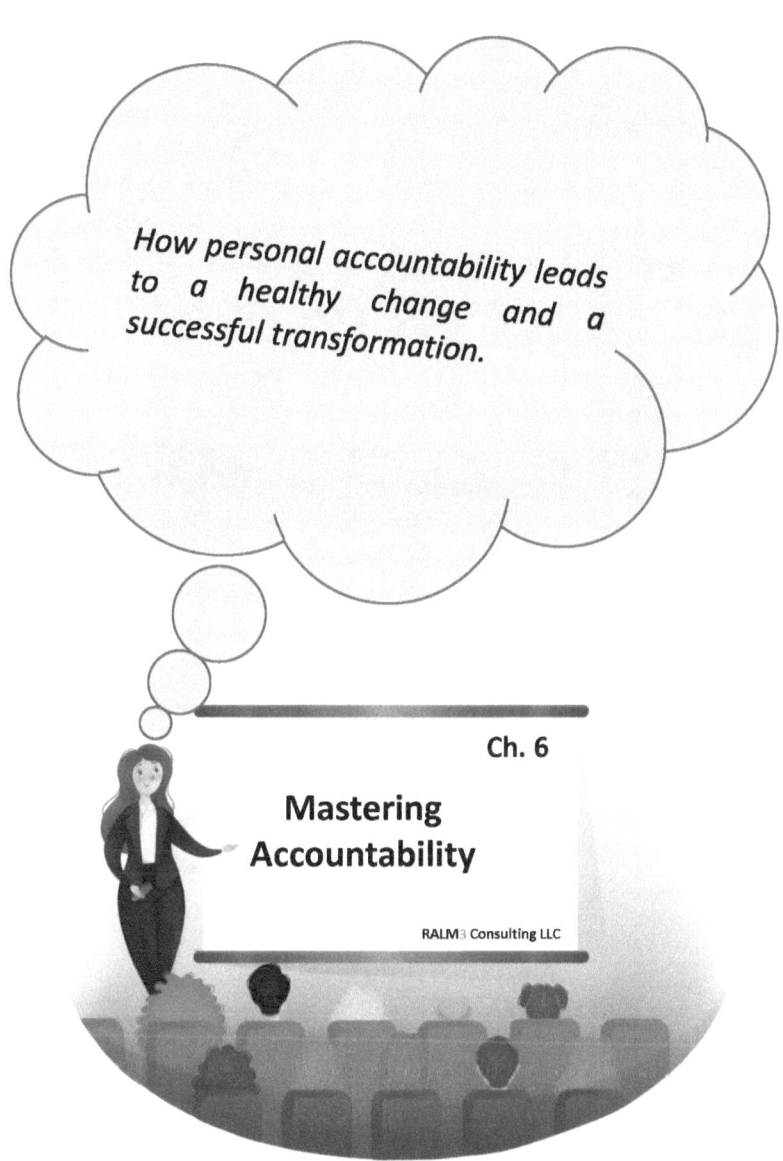

Illustration 6a. Mastering Accountability

About the Stories in this Chapter

"If you think about your own person as a brand and as such, what perception would you portray? Do you want to be perceived as unreliable, not trustworthy, etc.? Would you like to be treated the same way you treat others? How would you feel if people didn't respond to your requests, ignored you, came late to meetings or didn't show up at all without letting you know? Also, if your manager or organization considered these unreliable approaches as a norm why wouldn't you? Culture and leadership are key... People follow their leaders, good or bad... Unfortunately. There are such things as group thinking, peer pressure that play a huge role in culture and surroundings that add to lack of accountability."

Natalie Vinitsky
Dynamic Change Agent | Contributing Author

If I have to be honest in answering "What is one thing that drives me absolutely bananas?" it would be people making promises and then not owning up to them. I talk and write a lot about having an extremely positive outlook on life (check out all the testimonials at beginning of my memoir "Life Worth Living") and being able to stay calm in the most stressful situation but let me tell you, nothing gets my blood boiling more than someone not delivering on their commitment. Blaming others would have to be second in line but this chapter focuses first and foremost on accountability. We talk about personal accountability, accountability for the culture of the organization as well accountability for a digital transformation. This chapter has the most quotes, exercises, and thought-provoking questions out of this whole book. I highly recommend you not skip any of the exercises, self-reflect and perhaps even get some action items going for yourself!

Illustration 6b. An organization's culture drives how people behave

6.1 Basic Expectations of Behavior

For a few months now, Vita had thought about getting a new bike. She had finally decided what she wanted, an Electra Townie Path 9D Step-Thru Cruiser. She was told by many of her friends that bikes are great to buy from Facebook Marketplace. She decided that since she knew exactly what she wanted, she might as well see what was out there. She came across a posting that displayed a like-new bike with all the bells and whistles for half the price it would be in a store, and they didn't even have them in stock! The only catch was it was an hour and a half drive. She debated just how much of a pain it would be but decided that she really wanted that bike, and she was willing to spend three hours in the car for it.

"What is the earliest that works on your side tomorrow morning?" Vita asked Donna via Facebook messenger, the only way to really communicate when going through Marketplace ads.

"Let me know what your preference is, and we will take it from there!" Donna replied.

"Well, I can be there as early as 7am but I understand it is a Sunday," Vita tried to be considerate even though she really wanted to avoid Cape Cod traffic and be back before her family even got a chance to miss her.

"How is 8:30 am?" Donna messaged back.

"It works! I will see you tomorrow at 8:30am. Please let me know if anything changes by 6:30am!" Vita confirmed.

Vita had arrived the following morning by 8:15am. But after waiting for 1.5 hours, Vita's blood was starting to boil a little. Vita was known for her empathy and having a positive outlook on life and all, but her patience was being tested. As much as she wanted to be understanding, she couldn't figure out how someone could just "forget." She knew she wasn't a saint herself and had forgotten things plenty of times before, but this seemed like a common courtesy. If you agreed to meet, set two alarm clocks and three reminders if you think there might be a possibility of you forgetting. She snapped out of it quickly though, telling herself that she shouldn't be so judgmental. After all, we are all different, with our own strengths and weaknesses and we should not assume or expect things from people just because they seem like a no brainer to us. Or should we?

Should we come up with a basic common agreement when interacting with each other, expressing what is important to us and what we are not willing to compromise with?

When Vita arrived at the address Donna gave her and let Donna know she had arrived, there was no reply. Messenger was the only way for them to communicate. They didn't exchange phone numbers and since they weren't friends on Facebook, Vita couldn't call Donna either.

"That's alright," Vita thought to herself. "I will give it 10 min."

After 15 min, seeing that Donna hadn't even read Vita's message, Vita messaged Donna again saying that she was going over to Starbucks to get breakfast and that hopefully Donna would get back to her before 9am. Vita didn't feel comfortable ringing the doorbell, just in case Donna had someone in the house asleep. She would hate to wake someone up, even Donna herself.

After Vita still hadn't heard anything and saw that none of her messages had even been read, she messaged again asking if Donna changed her mind or overslept. She was less upset but more disappointed that not only did she just drive for an hour and a half, but she was also about to turn back without the bike she really wanted. What a wasted three hours of the weekend. Vita decided to go get gas and swing by Donna's place again, just in case. As she was standing by her car, debating whether she should ring the doorbell or just head back, she caught herself thinking, *how can one be so unreliable? Where is accountability? Does this woman behave the same at work?*

Vita continued her thought process with, *what if Donna was up all night with little kids and it just slipped her mind? It is unlikely but it is a possibility. It is the weekend, it is not her routine...*

Vita was extremely annoyed but at the same time, being a mother of young children herself not so long ago, she could somewhat understand and justify this lack of common courtesy. Vita started walking towards the door and noticed the TV was on through the window blinds. It was 10am. She had driven for 1.5 hours and had been waiting for 1.5 hours. She really wanted the bike and so she rang the doorbell. An 11-year-old boy opened the door and with suspicion and curiosity listened to Vita explaining what she was there for. To Vita's relief, he said, "Oh, that's right...about the bike...one second." He called to his mom.

"I am sorry, I forgot!" Donna said immediately as she opened the door.

As Vita was driving back with the bike in her car, she reflected on the situation. What she first considered a lack of common courtesy and accountability turned out to be a young mom's sleepless night. Was that still considered a lack of accountability, or it is something else if there is a justifiable excuse?

Vita pondered that question and then discussed it with a few of her colleagues in the following weeks.

"What does it mean in general to be accountable?" Vita asked Asmita as they were discussing a bigger topic of quality accountability. "What causes the lack of accountability?"

As Asmita dove into sharing examples from her past, they discussed how important it is to take pride in the work you do. They talked about Type B personalities who don't necessarily go above and beyond and choose to just do the bare minimum. They talked about the importance of understanding the "why" behind the work employees are being asked to do and how the connection of what they do to the bigger purpose could influence enthusiasm.

"Honestly," said Vita, "I am not even sure if it is related to one loving their job or not. Isn't it just work ethic? I might not enjoy what I am doing in any given moment, but that doesn't mean I ignore a deadline or just throw half ass work over the wall, right?"

We do need to understand the root cause as much as possible, but at the end of the day, it is ok to expect people to be accountable for the promises they make or the work they take on. We can help each other by offering constructive feedback but we can't force someone to behave one way or another. People have to be self-aware and accountable for their commitments.

6.2 Solving the Right Problem

"This is extremely frustrating," Vita shared. "I understand that people have different levels of passion for the work they do, and it is not about Type A personalities, I am talking about accountability. It is not just about taking pride in the work you do but having respect for the people you work with. What makes someone just ignore a deadline and not even mention that they don't plan on delivering what they committed to? More than that, when asked, they blame it on other teams. It is always someone else's fault. There is a pattern now that I am observing."

"Listen," said Olivia with a very calm voice. She could tell Vita was boiling inside. "Lack of accountability does often become a blame game, but I think we often fail to recognize that the word itself, the meaning of accountability, could be interpreted and internalized differently for different people. So, individual behavior comes from each person's own definition of accountability."

"That's an interesting thought," Vita said, now a lot calmer than before. "It seems so straightforward to me. If you say you will do something, you get it done. I guess this is my definition of accountability. I like things simple."

"I hear you, but because it's such a vague or multidimensional word, it causes misalignment among people, which in turn causes frustration and often conflict. I often say don't go blaming, resolve any conflict you may have by getting people in the room, well Zoom these days, and understand what's the lowest common denominator, because it is always there," Olivia paused for a second noticing that Vita was not quite following.

"Do you mind diving in a bit into the last thing you said? What do you mean by finding the common denominator?" Vita asked.

"Sure, so I think accountability can be built up. How can we find that overlap of what the common grounds are? What is that level of shared understanding of what we're trying to accomplish? How am I going to contribute to that goal? How are you going to contribute to that goal? When we come to a shared understanding, we can then capture these artifacts."

"Interesting that we go back to the topic of alignment." Vita said.

"Right, so to me, we often jump to conflict resolution but that's the wrong problem to solve because it is an artificial conflict. It is possible that there is no conflict. We just need to find a shared truth and spend more time doing that," Olivia continued, and Vita had a major aha moment.

"Funny you should say that. I pay so much attention to conflict resolution and talk a lot about achieving organizational alignment, but these two topics are very much connected to a lack of accountability. It sounds like to master accountability we need to focus first and foremost on achieving organizational alignment and the rest might just fall into place."

"Exactly. We need to make sure we are solving the root cause of the real problem rather than a symptom," Olivia concluded.

"It makes total sense," Vita agreed. "It reminds me of the example you shared with me earlier when you were solving employee dissatisfaction but had to really distill it into what exactly you were going to solve since dissatisfaction is very personal and subjective."

"Right, and because it was a big hairy ball, we needed to synthesize everyone's input, decide on the four things we were going to make better and not rush into the solution, not rush into execution. We had to give it enough time to double-check with the right stakeholders that we were addressing the right problem. We needed to change the perception of our organization, but we needed to first agree among the executive team what we were going to focus on and how we were going to measure if we were making a difference," Olivia added.

"Sounds like you and I can talk for hours about this stuff," Vita said realizing they needed to wrap up.

"Indeed, we can!" said Olivia with a smile.

6.3 Who is Accountable for Culture?

"Small changes that are about tools or fairly insulated processes may not require a change to the culture, but a large-scale transformation absolutely will. These usually require people to think very differently about how they work — maybe they are shifting from using a complicated approval process involving different groups to one that is more self-service. This can require groups or individuals to take on a much greater level of accountability than what they have in the past. That has a significant impact on their behaviors and how they think and plan for their work."

Jennifer Greve
Transformation Specialist | Contributing Author

Vita posted a question about personal accountability in a group channel with all the contributing authors, who were experts in different areas, from product managers to executive coaches, quality experts, to digital transformation leaders. She had paused to watch how the discussion unfolded and appreciated the collective knowledge, skills, experience, and passion for the topic. The discussion was very fruitful with lots of opinions, bold statements, a bit of disagreement and even sarcastic clarifications. It is a dream of any facilitator when instead of just observing and waiting for someone else to say something, participants are triggered, and passion just starts pouring out.

"There is a lot of wisdom in this conversation. Let me ask another question, "Who is accountable for the culture then?" We often hear disappointment as far as company culture and for whatever reason, everyone thinks that someone else is responsible for whatever the culture is lacking, bringing us back to the topic of personal accountability. What are your thoughts on that?" Vita loved this type of discussion. They weren't sitting across the same desk in a conference room, but the discussion wasn't less impactful.

Transforming culture is extremely important and it is in fact very difficult, so how does one go about it? Who is accountable for the culture?

"The CEO is responsible for the culture," one of the contributing authors chimed in.

"Are you serious or being sarcastic?" Vita had to clarify.

"I was serious about CEOs being responsible for the culture. It is fragile and needs full support and commitment top down. CEOs need to lead by example."

Then another contributing author chimed in, "Leadership is critical in defining the culture they want and establishing the structures and policies to support it but then it becomes the responsibility of everyone to make it real. Culture is reflected in how you approach business operations, define incentives and promotion guidelines, what you look for in job candidates, etc. The problem often comes because culture is allowed to evolve organically, and the structures can erode over time, so they no longer reflect a cohesive whole. Think what happens when budgets get cut so staffing changes are made that limit opportunity for growth. How often does leadership take the time to look beyond the numbers for the ways to maintain the culture?"

Vita couldn't help but continue to think about her original statement/question, "Everyone thinks that someone else is responsible for whatever the culture is lacking but what about personal accountability?"

It seems that when it comes to culture and accountability there is often some kind of blame in the air. It is always someone else's fault. Vita wasn't disagreeing that it has to start at the top and executives need to lead by example, but there was just something that kept bugging her. Who, if not the individual, is accountable for their own personal growth and to find ways to contribute to the culture they are part of? This question led Vita to come up with a few exercises for a workshop on accountability. There is a way to relay a message to someone who may need a reminder in a non-threatening way. Having folks just read the quotes (to maybe have those aha moments without having to voice it) is a great way to get those thoughts going in hopes that it will resonate.

6.3.1 Exercise

Which of the quotes below speak to you the most?

1) *"I think that sometimes the root of the problem is unrealistic goal setting. If everyone knows in advance that what is planned cannot be accomplished, they are a lot less interested in performing. So sometimes even less is achieved than it would be if expectations were set correctly."*

2) *"Does not delivering on milestones add to job security? And if it's not possible, why not raise it? It's all about culture. If people feel psychologically safe to raise issues, they feel more included and thus accountable."*

3) *"Culture is the key, but goal setting is a part of culture."*

4) *"If leaders provide clear communication (and maybe even inspiration) on what they need to achieve, explain "why" and leave to their teams "how" they are going to do it with the promise to help timely remove obstacles anything will be possible. The culture without politics and "what's in it for us as a team and organization" vs "me" is the key. To achieve this, leaders need to provide corresponding "incentives" that will drive behavior and thus culture."*

5) *"Lack of decision making that comes from the leaders and avoidance of personal responsibility is the cause of most pain points. Cultural transformation is the most important and difficult"*

6.3.2 Exercise

Accountability for a growth mindset: Which quote speaks the most to you?

1) *"The word accountability itself threatens people if they are not given proper tools, knowledge, incentives and in general are set for success."*

2) *"What if they were given the tools, training, incentives but they are still not motivated and don't feel accountable for anything, even their own learning?"*

3) *"Does one need to be told to be accountable or does it come from the culture and thus how you feel?"*

4) *"When I am told "you are accountable for X," I feel like walking away thinking that if something goes wrong, I will be blamed. **I do more when I feel inspired and empowered.**"*

5) *"Holding people accountable without empowering them does not work and will create a reaction of walking away. For example, if the product owner is accountable for quality or DevOps or any function but is not empowered to change or make investments in those organizations, how can they be fully accountable for the function?"*

6) *"Culture of empowerment comes first, as others have pointed out. But there still has to be an intrinsic internal accountability or drive in each individual. We do need to own our shit in the end. Each individual takes responsibility for the work they do, for their own growth, for how they treat others etc. No external factor (culture, CEO, etc.), no matter how inspiring, will move an individual if they are not intrinsically motivated."*

7) *"Just to circle back to those cases where people were given everything they need to be successful, and they're still not doing what's expected, perhaps they are not in the right job. Unfortunately, given the statistics more than 90% people really don't like what they're doing and that could be the issue. So perhaps the culture and leadership are about finding the right spot or a good area for people to work and the accountability will come along."*

8) *"There are many folks who used to like what they did but the job changed and then they didn't. And I agree that a lot of that comes naturally when people are engaged in what they do."*

9) *"If people take pride in what they do, personal accountability comes naturally. If not, you cannot force people to be accountable, just empower and inspire them, but the fire has to be from within."*

6.4 Who is Accountable for a Successful Digital Transformation?

"An organization's culture drives how people behave. This can include formal components like vision and values, but it also includes the unwritten, often unspoken, "how we do business." Large organizations typically have different cultures across different departments. It can be important to take this into consideration when planning enterprise level transformations or change initiatives that span groups.

Jennifer Greve
Transformation Specialist | Contributing Author

About a decade into entering the world of agile, Vita started questioning more and more reasons behind certain decisions, practices and overall goals when engaging with clients. Understanding the WHY behind the WHAT not only affects accountability and engagement of folks who are doing the work, but it can affect prioritization of the work and efficiency with which the higher-level goals are achieved. She found the following two questions effective in peeling the onion of potential areas for improvement:

Question #1. What does success look like?
Question #2. How will we know it was a success?

The first question Vita borrowed from a book called *Dare to Lead* by Brene Brown, who is known for her research on vulnerability and how it is connected to leadership skills. The second question was paraphrased but based on the work of John Doerr mentioned in Chapter 5 when talking about measuring what matters, as well as OKRs.

In section 3.7, as well as section 5.8, we discussed the concept of "Backlog Is the Boss" as part of the organizational alignment in the context of a digital transformation. When the vision for the transformation is set and the backlog for the transformation is created, the right measures are in place and it is very clear to all what success looks like and how we will know it was a success, there may be work items in that backlog for the CEO, for the head of HR, for an engineering lead or for a coach. The work items could in fact include behavior changes, leadership skills in this new way of working along with ways to measure those as well. It is not all about process and there isn't a single person who could be accountable for the success of the digital transformation. However, there is a ton of personal accountability that has to take place in order for all of it to add up to a successful digital transformation!

6.5 Exercise

Prepare for a Workshop to Define Working Agreement, Decision Making, and Ownership

1. What behaviors do we need to exhibit and how do we need to work together in order for the transformation to be successful?

2. What current behaviors and cultural norms would be detrimental to positive organizational change?

3. How can we encourage behaviors and practices we need and let go of the ones that may slow down our transformation?

4. Let's discuss how we want to make decisions. Remember that pushing decision making down the organizational chain speeds up change. What type of decisions will require a consensus at a higher level and what types of decisions can be made by the individual teams?

5. Now let's look at our top transformation objectives (or goals, or outstanding action items). Do we have a clear owner for each? And does each owner have enough influence over their objective/goal/action item to move it forward?

6. What changes do we need to implement to ensure objective owners have the right level of influence in their areas of accountability?

Illustration 6c. Importance of Personal Accountability

CHAPTER 7

Maximizing Value Delivered

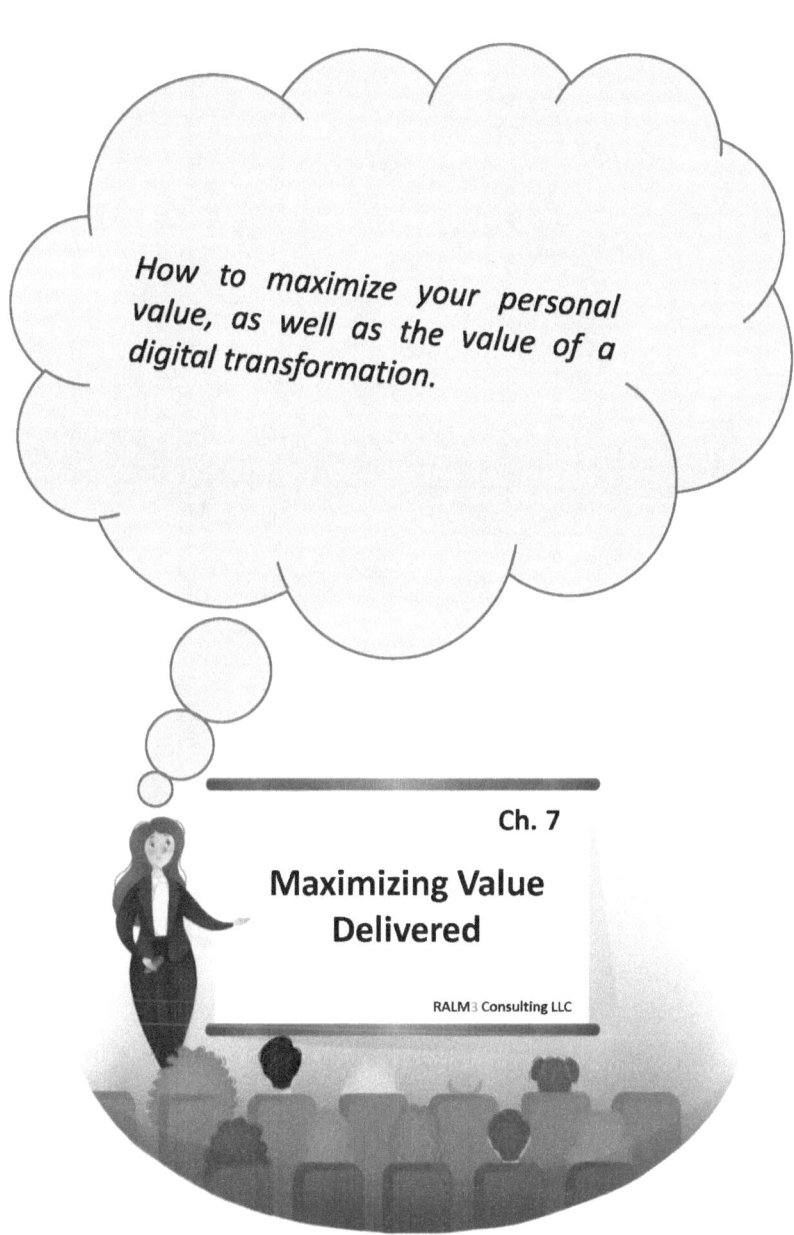

Illustration 7a. Maximizing Value Delivered

About the Stories in this Chapter

"Clear definition of who your current customers are and what customers you are trying to target in the future leads to design customer experience from outside in. If the goal of digital transformation is to improve customer experience and provide personalization, every effort of digital transformation needs to start with understanding and diagnostics of customer needs. Don't go to your customers (current and future) with empty hands - provide them with thoughts and options that you want to validate."

Tatiana Thomas
Director of Customer Experience and Digital Strategy | Contributing Author

Just as we like to ask the question "Why change?" when it comes to any agile or digital transformation, no matter how large or small, we also find it very effective to ask a question "Who is this for?" and "What value does it bring?" and, last but not least, "How do you maximize that value?"

We first start by defining the value. It is a theme throughout the book to not make assumptions, define exactly what it is you are talking about and only then begin peeling the onion. We can think of value in the context of the solution we are developing, service we provide or the role we play.

This chapter discusses value as customer-facing (external), as well as employee-facing (internal). We share a story where we walk the reader through a value definition workshop, as well as give an example of how one can maximize their value as a product owner. We continue with sharing stories on the topic of maximizing value as a coach, as a leader and a change agent. We share an interview with a founder of a startup company which focuses on maximizing internal value with AI bots automation and finish off discussing what it takes to actually maximize the value of a digital transformation.

Illustration 7b. The impact of digital transformation on challenges of the future

7.1 What is Value?

"What is value and who are your customers?" Vita asked the million-dollar question during leadership training at a new engagement.

"Are you talking about external customers?" a voice from Zoom spoke up.

"Great question! Before we dive a bit more into this topic, let me ask you, if at all possible, to turn your cameras on. In this case, you are my customers and for me, to bring the most value to you as a trainer, I need to see if I am putting you to sleep or saying something inspiring," Vita asked politely but gave a pretty firm message that it is in their interest to turn their cameras on. "I also get a lot more energy from the audience than from the green light of my camera, so it is really in your interest."

When the majority of the training attendees turned their cameras on, Vita returned to the topic of external customers.

"Let's explore the external customers for now," said Vita. "Who uses the solution this company develops? Have you gone through the exercise of defining **personas**?"

"What are personas?" someone asked.

"Anyone want to take a stab at answering?" Vita offered but got no volunteers.

They dove into specific personas after Vita explained that personas are fictional characters you create based on your research that represent the folks who will use your service, product, solution, or a platform. Creating personas helps you understand your users' experiences, behaviors, needs and goals.

"Now, let me ask you a question. Who are your internal customers?" Vita continued.

Someone from the infrastructure team immediately said that for them, everyone in the company is their customer.

"So, in your case, how would you define delivering value?" Vita said.

"Ensuring uptime? Well, we can't often calculate the return on investment when we are up all night making sure our production systems stay up, but I guess we can still calculate the cost based on what company might lose each hour our systems are down."

"Great! Makes sense...anyone else want to add?" Vita wanted to make sure everyone's voice was heard.

After a few other contributions to the discussion, Vita continued, "Let's put the financial gain or loss of the company aside for a second. How else can we define delivering value to the customers, internal or external? What other dimensions can we think of other than financial?"

"Usability?" someone offered.

"Reputation?" someone else picked up.

"That's right!" Vita said. "There are many ways we can define value and we often talk about value when we prioritize work. The concept of personas and value is applicable not only in the context of external product delivery, but also improving internal processes, increasing employee engagement and so much more. Product owners, who are on the hook to make decisions about what work teams should focus on, think about VALUE all the time. Now, how about bringing value as a Leader? What does that mean to you?"

Since this training was all about leadership and how their role changes when they move away from individual contributors, it was essential to dive into the specifics of what leading meant for them. Vita knew from her own experience that when you move from the hands-on engineering work and become a manager, a leader, and a coach, it is often hard to understand what value you bring to the table, because in your mind, you may still think that if you haven't written any code or created an artifact of some sort, then you really hadn't done much. That's when many leaders tend to go back to that hands-on work rather supporting their people, mentoring, and growing their people's skills.

They discussed how growing their people, empowering them to make decisions and creating an environment where people feel comfortable speaking up and asking for help will allow them to scale and in return, maximize value they can actually deliver!

7.2 Value Definition Workshop

"What if you create a ton of value but nobody is willing to pay for it? Is that still a success?" Someone from the audience asked.

"Well, it depends on how value is defined," said Vita.

Vita shared her screen, where she had a few sticky notes written out on a virtual white board with some tangible benefits a business could get from a product or a solution and asked everyone to add at least one additional sticky note to the ones already there (revenue growth, expense reduction and outage penalties).

"How are we doing?" Vita asked. She saw a few new sticky notes added to the Mural board (a popular virtual board for engaging workshops) but not nearly as many as she had hoped.

"What else? Would we only consider the financial aspect, or can value be represented in something other than dollars?"

There was dead silence and while Vita was trained as a facilitator to be comfortable with silence in order to get more people to participate, she decided to proceed, "Ok, let's first focus on all that can be measured in dollars." After a few minutes, the Mural board was populated with the following:

1. Lost Revenue
2. Increased Expenses
3. Total Cost of Ownership
4. Return on Investment

5. Cycle Time Reduction
6. SLA Penalties

"This is great!" Vita said. "Let me ask you a question. What is something all of your teams measure these days and whether they should or should not, the leadership team actually pays a lot of attention to?"

"Are you talking about velocity?" Kevin bravely went off mute, for which Vita was extremely grateful.

"Yes! That's exactly what I had in mind. If you think about a certain effort, say improving deployment process, which would increase team velocity, would that be considered business value? Feel free to type yes or no in the chat if you prefer to stay on mute."

After all of the participants who chose to answer typed "yes" in the chat and a few folks went off mute to share their opinion on the topic, Vita was ready for the second exercise and asked folks to think now about intangible business value. She set the timer to three minutes and soon the board was populated with the following:

1. Company Reputation
2. Customer Satisfaction
3. Employee Satisfaction
4. Legal Compliance
5. Product Safety
6. Regulatory Compliance
7. Risk Avoidance
8. Risk Mitigation
9. Maintenance (Support, Bug Fixes, etc.)

The next exercise in this workshop was to list all work that is currently IN PROGRESS, as well as the WISH list — objectives that hadn't made the top 10 list but were still very much desirable. This is where the most value of the workshop began. An open discussion among product owners and leadership where they dove into the specifics of the work in progress and the true challenges that were holding them back.

"We are barely keeping our heads above water and constantly putting out fires. We need to invest in our infrastructure and internal processes. Otherwise, it is very difficult to innovate. It definitely doesn't help with employee satisfaction, not to mention revenue growth or customer satisfaction."

"That's right. So, as product owners, it is helpful to see this visual of all that's on the table and all that you would want to do, the wish list, and discuss with your teams and your leadership team what has to happen in order for the organization to get there. When your teams talk about "technical debt" and you have a healthy argument that you need more features, think about long term success too. They might find it difficult to articulate the business value of the technical work they are asking to prioritize but it is worth diving in and tying it all together. **When they talk about "cloud" for example and what needs to happen in order to scale infrastructure, it is important to understand that unless that is prioritized over short-term quick gains, there is only so far you will be able to go in the future."**

7.3 Maximizing Value as a Product Owner

Vita was sitting in an open cafeteria, grabbing lunch with a newly hired product owner and another colleague of hers, Nellie. They were talking about roles and responsibilities of product owners and discussed how in some companies, a product manager or even a chief product owner sets the vision for where the company needs to go and, in some companies, the product owner is accountable to set the vision and translate that vision into user stories, or chunks of work that would be consumable by the delivery team. Once again, Vita found herself listening to one of the new product owners expressing his concerns with how well he is doing in his new role.

"See, I don't know if I just don't have the right skills or I am stretched too thin, but I have a hard time prioritizing work for the team and for that matter, even deciding what work we should be focusing on. I can work with the team, but when I am asked to create a backlog without the opportunity to interact with real customers or do any market research, I am not sure how I can be expected to actually make strategic decisions," said Peter.

"Nellie, you used to be a product owner, didn't you?" Vita asked. "What are your thoughts on interacting with customers to be able to set the vision for what to build?"

"Oh, my goodness! Are you sure you want to get me started on this?" Nellie laughed.

She then shared her colorful experience being a product owner back in the day. The story was about being persistent in the desire to delight customers and not being afraid to interact with them directly. Nellie described how she had included her whole development team in the ideation stage and how engaged they were, which led to undeniable success. Nellie was telling the story with a ton of passion and Vita suggested Nellie shared it in more details as a great case study. Nellie did put it in writing eventually but for the time being, Peter did get value out of the shorter version of it during lunch.

> *Only six weeks after our chief digital officer (CDO) drew a sketch on a white board, our brand-new mobile app was live in both app stores, Apple and Google. The six-week marathon that we sprinted at break-neck speeds seemed like a surreal adventure. But we did not even know that it was only the beginning.*

> *I took the job of the mobile app product manager in early September of 2017, transitioning out of IT and into digital at the same company, a national big box retailer with over 200 large brick and mortar stores up and down the East Coast. Digital was a new organization that had just been spun up a few weeks earlier, tasked with a very ambitious goal of taking the traditional retailer into the digital space in under a year.*

> *Like many other brick-and-mortar retailers in 2017, we were falling behind the market in enabling a true Omni experience where a customer could choose whatever channel they preferred to shop with us - website, mobile, or a physical store, while also seamlessly transitioning between these modalities. We did not even have a mobile app.*

> *Our new CDO was an ambitious visionary, not hindered by the weight of realities of our systems limitations. Large parts of our systems were still running on the mainframe.*

> *The CDO wanted to make a splash by getting our brand-new mobile app out to market in six weeks and it had to be "sticky."*

Maximizing Value Delivered

We needed something that would make people come back to the app over and over. The new app was meant to be the harbinger of our new digital capabilities that were promising to boost eCommerce in addition to brick-and-mortar sales. The overhaul of the eCommerce site and the order management system (OMS) were going to take a few months, so the new mobile app was going to become the teaser and a way to start changing our brand perception to more digitally advanced. Our primary customer was aging with the company. We needed to start developing our customer's digital habits. The app had to be very simple and user friendly.

As our shopper's children were growing up and moving out, our customers' shopping baskets were shrinking. Bad news for a big box retailer. We wanted to also become attractive to younger growing families. And for that we needed to enable our digital channels.

The team got together to brainstorm what would be a quick win but would provide enough value to the customer so that they would keep coming back to the app. We wanted to start changing our brand's perception as early as possible, while we continued working on the overhaul of the rest of our systems and powering up our e-commerce and Omni capabilities. We needed a quick Minimum Viable Product (MVP) that would be sticky enough that we could continue to add features to.

I started our first brainstorming session with a challenge to the team. "Team, we need to be really creative. I want to hear all ideas, no matter how crazy or simple. We have six weeks before Black Friday when we want our app to be out in the market. What can we do in this timeframe that would be simple but sticky?"

"Can you explain what you mean by sticky?" Keith, the freshly appointed mobile app developer asked.

"It needs to provide value, such that the shopper would keep coming back to the app."

"The first thing that comes to mind is repeated purchases, like paper towels," one of the developers said.

"General grocery is not yet enabled through order management. We have to build out a bunch of APIs for that. That's on the roadmap for next year," Raj was on the OMS team and knew what was going on there.

"So, what do we sell online now?"

"Mostly big-ticket items, like electronics and furniture."

"Yeah, I don't think that's something you'd be buying very often."

I had to chime in. "Online shopping in general needs to wait until the eCommerce overhaul. We don't have the APIs to let the app connect directly to the OMS. We would have to just cram existing website pages inside the app. That would be ugly."

"How about some general information about the stores? Like address and store hours."

"Yes, that should be easy! That data all just sits in one table and feeds the store locator on the website. We can build a simple API for that. Not sure this is sticky enough though. I mean, how often do you look up the store hours?"

"What about membership information? Like the membership expiration date and rewards."

Everyone turned to Alison, who was representing the membership team at the table.

Maximizing Value Delivered

"Some of the basic data should be available, we display that on the website now."

"Do you know if there is an API?"

"Yes, we have a very basic one. Like expiration date and awards."

"It would be awesome if we could show how much our members have saved. Do you have that data?"

"We do, we include it in our quarterly letters. But it's not exposed to the API."

"Ok, so far we have a store locator and basic membership information. What else?"

Everyone got quiet.

"Hey, you know that app, Gas Buddy? You can see real time gas prices. Can we do something like that?"

"That's a great idea. Most of our stores have gas stations and with our competitive prices this would be a great feature."

"Awesome, now my favorite question. Do we have an API for that?" I asked.

"Let me ping Abishek in Middleware. Keep talking for now."

"What else guys? You shop in our stores, anything you could use an app for?"

"One of the pain points that keeps coming up in customer complaints to the call center is having to carry the membership card around. Can we put the membership barcode on the app?"

"Yes, we can! That one is pretty easy, we have the membership ID from Alison. And there are libraries out there to turn that into a barcode."

"Not so fast guys. There is an issue. Most of our self check-out lanes are not equipped with the right scanners. They cannot read a barcode off a phone screen. We tried that with the in-store scan and go project. Our gas pumps also need an upgrade of their scanners. It's on the roadmap within the next three years.

We did this research for another project. If we put a barcode in the app, it will generate more frustration and customer complaints than benefit. It's really not a good idea."

"That's a bummer. That would've been a low hanging fruit and great value to our members."

"Ok, I just confirmed with Abishek. They use a third-party application for gas price management, and it's enabled for APIs, we just need to set it up."

"Fantastic, so that's three now. Locator, membership, gas prices. What else guys?"

"How about coupons?" Sarah piped up. "We just enabled digital coupons on our website, it was a massive project. Adoption is really skyrocketing. We are adding hundreds of adopters each week. We are still ironing out some kinks, but in general it's very successful. Can we do anything with that?"

"Brilliant, Sarah! I know for a fact that the digital coupons vendor has a robust API system. I can't believe we did not think of this earlier. That's a perfect feature to incentivize digital habits in our members. They would literally be paid to use the app. So far, we have a store locator, membership, gas prices, and digital coupons.

Maximizing Value Delivered

You guys rock! Now we need to figure out how feasible it is to do this all in six weeks."

I looked at Keith. Keith looked very serious. "Well, we do have that app development agency we will use. They will take care of all the app stuff; we just need to make sure we get all our internal APIs sorted out with the Middleware team and the coupons vendor. This will be very tight."

Everyone got quiet.

It was indeed very tight. Those six weeks were one of the most intense periods of my career, with all hands-on deck for many long days and nights. The team pulled together beautifully, in just a couple of 2-week sprints we built a brand-new app that was integrated with three different internal systems (membership, gas prices, and a store locator) and an external digital coupons system.

To say we were ecstatic when the app launched by the Black Friday rush and downloads started picking up, would have been an understatement.

And then the reality set in. Our app ratings were just awful. We were barely getting two out of five, on average. Something was horribly wrong, and we needed to figure it out fast and fix it.

What we needed was customer feedback. From our perspective the app was a perfect MVP, it had a few useful but simple features, and it had the stickiness of the digital coupons. Obviously, our end users disagreed.

I started sifting through the app ratings and reviews. There were a few 4- and even 5-star reviews saying how useful the new app was. Some users even mentioned they had been waiting for our app for a long time. But then there were a lot of 1-star reviews that brought our average down to below 2. Those reviews were very short "Does not work," "It's ridiculous, I cannot even log in," "Fire these developers," "Piece of crap." It was not a whole lot to go on, but one thing became clear - there was a serious bug that was preventing many users from logging into the app even for the first time.

Our developers were pouring over logs, trying to find what the problem was. They found a couple of bugs and fixed them, but it did not seem to help our ratings at all.

At the same time our CDO was eager to get our show on the road. He wanted us to start promoting the new mobile app in the stores, so that both our store associates and customers became familiar with it. We were going to raffle off a few gift cards for those who downloaded the app.

As a product manager, I was supposed to go to app launch events in our largest stores and I felt uneasy. I knew the app was not working for many people and having a flop on our first road show did not seem like a lot of fun. Interestingly, I was wrong! The event at our flagship store in New York City was in fact a lot of fun, despite the snowstorm outside! I was paired up with a marketing professional who seemed to make friends with even the grumpiest of New Yorkers walking in from the storm outside. And yes, we had a few users that could not log into the app. I was able to watch closely over their shoulder and realized that our login process had a few flaws. It was too cumbersome and seemed to kick some users out at the end, after they had entered all their membership information. This is when a lot of people gave up, deleted the app, and gave us a 1-star rating.

I pleaded with two or three users to get on the phone with the customer service for me to troubleshoot. And when they did, I hit the jackpot. Turned out that if a user had a pre-existing online account but did not know their password (and most of our users rarely used their online accounts or did not even know they had one), after three unsuccessful attempts, their account locked up for security reasons, but nothing more than an obscure error code was given, and the user was left in total frustration and with no help. The customer service agent on the phone was able to unlock my users' accounts and reset their passwords. And they were off on their way, happily clipping their digital coupons.

When I came back to the headquarters, my first stop was at Danielle's office, who was the head of customer service. When Danielle heard the story of a call center agent resolving the issue in a couple of minutes, she immediately had an idea: "I think your team needs to solve this issue systemically, it's just too expensive to have every user call the customer services. But while you are working on a solution, can we direct customers with these issues to the call center right away? We can't have them be this frustrated."

"That would be fantastic. We can just update the error message to direct the user to call customer service. Actually, we should even put the phone number on the login screen."

"Let's put together an **SOP** for the call center. In case someone calls who cannot log into the app. We should also instruct the agents to report back on the app issues, so you have more customer feedback."

I promised Danielle we would also brainstorm a systemic solution with the app team. Very soon we had a plan. We were going to simplify our login screen and even allow for scanning of the membership barcode to pull up the customer data. We would also work with the cybersecurity team to optimize the password reset feature.

But first, we replaced that obscure error message with the customer service phone number. That was a quick fix that Keith pushed out that same day.

In the next two weeks we watched our app ratings slowly grow, together with the number of active users. We were now just above two in the Apple store. The customer service team was diligently reporting back on the issues daily.

Even with a more streamlined login process, we were still not out of the woods. Low app ratings were still coming in for all sorts of issues. Users would give the app 1 star even when they had an issue with a digital coupon not applying correctly at the store. And we could not act on that at all, because we needed to at least know the store, the product, and ideally the transaction ID from the receipt in order to troubleshoot. None of that was available from anonymous App Store reviews. We felt helpless. The idea of the app being a harbinger of the digital future was quickly becoming laughable. Something had to be done.

I was in Danielle's office again explaining how we had no direct access to our users with problems and unable to troubleshoot and therefore, fix the issues.

Danielle had another great idea: "What if we bifurcate the flow of the ratings?"

"What do you mean?"

"Have the happy users give us a rating on the app stores, but have the unhappy users contact our customer service. Then we can collect more information and actually solve their problems and fix the app."

"Love it! I am sure there is a way for us to do that."

My small and very agile team quickly had a solution out. We've identified a couple of moments in the app when we thought the users should be feeling productive, for example after they clipped a coupon. Then we would pop up a question "Do you love this app? Yes. No." Very simple. If they answered yes, we asked them to rate us on the App Store. If they answered no, then we asked them to fill out a quick complaint form for the customer service. We also added a bug report feature in the app, since we realized the App Store reviews was the only way for some of our users to voice their frustration.

The day the feedback feature went live was when emails started coming in. By then I was so hungry for actual users to give me enough information to solve their problems, I started corresponding with many users myself. Within a couple of weeks, we identified a good number of issues that we were able to fix and not just with the app. It turned out we had issues with some of the vendor coupons redeeming incorrectly, associates in some of the stores needed training on the mobile app and digital coupons. A handful of gas stations were not loading prices correctly. It was a whole host of low to medium severity bugs that were in the way of our users' delight.

We watched the app ratings grow and grow and reach over 4.5 in just another month. And my favorite part was when users who had left a 1-star rating would come back and change it to 5 stars, noting how happy they were with the customer service they received.

"WOW! What a story!" Vita exclaimed. "It is no wonder you remember it so vividly. It must have been very satisfying to see those customers who left a 1-star rating go back and change it to 5. That's pretty amazing!"

"This is very helpful, actually," said Peter and thanked Nellie for sharing her story. "I think part of my frustration comes from the fact that I keep thinking the whole backlog is on me and only me. I think I will schedule a brainstorming session with my team, invite a few other more senior product owners too and our architect. I mean, we do have a direction somewhat set for us, so it is not like I am going in completely blind. Maybe I need to schedule a one-on-one with my boss, confirm I understand the high-level direction and go from there."

"There you go!" Vita was happy with just how productive this lunch was. She made a mental note to herself to remember this moment in case she would question what value she actually brought that day as a coach.

7.4 Maximizing Value as a Coach

Just like in one of the previous chapters where Vita had a passionate discussion with someone about whether a computer science degree is necessary to succeed in a high-tech world, she found herself discussing on LinkedIn what makes a great coach. It was a poll with the following options to choose from:

a) Coach should have proper certifications
b) Coach should have a large following on LinkedIn
c) Depends on books read and/or written
d) Technical Background

Vita's first gut reaction was that she had seen really great coaches without any certifications and not so great ones with many certifications, degrees, books read and even a large following on LinkedIn. She continued to think about what makes a great coach and asked herself the following questions:

a) What reflects their emotional intelligence?
b) What about their ability to recognize that their style of coaching isn't a good fit for a particular team or organization and ability to adjust their style based on what will do the trick?
c) How can one tell if the coach has a growth mindset themselves?
d) Is the coach able to recognize where people are in their mindset and skills and meet them where they are?

When it comes to **Emotional Intelligence (EQ)**, you can read and even write a ton of books and still get triggered and behave in a way that may not be desirable in order to achieve desirable outcomes. It takes a lot of self-awareness and hard work to build up your EQ if it doesn't happen to be something that comes naturally to you. Coaches are people just like everyone else with their default communication styles, habits, and preferences, so adjusting to anything different takes effort, as well as a growth mindset.

As coaches become more and more experienced and some things start to seem a no-brainer, it is easy to fall into the trap of "Why don't they get it, it is so simple!?" It is important to always remember that for some people, it may be the first time they hear words like agile or scrum or cloud, so being a great coach also means meeting people where they are in their transformation journey.

Coaches also need to be self-aware and realize when they need to step out of a situation before making things worse for the client. As a career, coaches try to problem solve, navigate politics, listen to people's problems, grow leaders, and so much more. Taking care of their own emotional and mental stability is critical to be able to help others. This is true for any type of leader, but this is necessary for a coach's health, stress, and ability to avoid career burnout.

To maximize value as a coach, one should practice no judgment, be generous with empathy and continue to learn themselves knowing that growth mindset applies to them as well, not only the people they are coaching! And when it comes to emotional intelligence, they would have to lead by example in that department! Ability to self-reflect, give and receive feedback and truly care about people and the organization is essential for a coach to achieve those set objectives!

7.5 Maximizing Value as a Leader

The stories shared in this book are not in chronological order. This particular one, although shared in the very last chapter, actually happened at the start of Vita's leadership journey (around Chapter 1.3). We are talking about a time so far back, when Vita actually had to Google what it meant to be a leader!

"A leader is not who has got the title but whose office rug is all worn out," said a new executive named Larry, who joined Vita's company as a senior VP of strategy. He said it to Vita with a smile during their first one-on-one. It was a compliment referring to the fact that there were always people near Vita's cubicle.

"I see people always stopping by your cubicle with questions and you are always willing to help," Larry continued.

Vita caught herself thinking about her first day on the job:

> "We have a few options for you to choose from as far as the workspace." Vita was given a quick tour on her first day in the office. There wasn't that much to show but it was the most beautiful space she had worked in by that point in her career. She had seen the open space with glass door conference rooms and a small kitchen area with a large TV when she came in earlier as a guest speaker. The office was on the top floor of a fancy building across from the Boston Tea Party and Children's museums.

"This seat is open if you like," offered the recruiter who was in the office that day appointed to greet Vita and show her around. She sounded a bit guilty.

"I know it is not the best, since you have the whole executive team behind you and everyone will walk by you all the time and your monitor is facing the corridor, which is annoying. So, let me show you one more, tucked in the back in the corner... we were saving it just for you!" she smiled.

"Oh, no need! Thank you!" Vita replied. "This one is perfect!"

Vita knew at this point in her career that to be an effective scrum master or an agile coach, she would have to be easily accessible to people. What better way than to sit right in the middle of the office, where people walk by you all day long. It was literally on the way from the entrance to any point in the office, from any point of the office to the bathroom, from entrance to the kitchen, from kitchen to the exit...you couldn't go anywhere without passing by Vita's cubicle.

Vita replied to Larry, "Oh, it is really just because of where I sit!"

"It is not just that Vita," Larry insisted. "You are a true leader."

"Thank you," Vita replied, without knowing what she is supposed to do next with that information. She went back to her cubicle and searched, **"What do Leaders do?"**

Seven years have gone by since that Google search. Now Vita was searching for an inspiring video by Simon Sinek to include in the leadership training she was designing for a client. She ended up training hundreds of leaders on what it meant to bring value as a leader.

Maximizing Value Delivered

As Simon Sinek defines it, "A leader's job is not to do the work for others, it's to help others figure out how to do it themselves, to get things done, and to succeed beyond what they thought possible."

Sometimes it is truly easier to do the work yourself, especially if one believes they will do a better job and faster. If we promote folks to leadership roles because they shine in their previous roles but don't provide support and teach them what it means to now bring value as a leader, it can lead to disappointment, and frustration for all parties involved. New leaders need support so they learn how to add value by growing others; by helping them succeed beyond what they thought possible.

7.6 Maximizing Internal Value with Automation

The topic of automation and the stories Vita could share about it could be a book on its own. We haven't talked at all yet about **infrastructure**, **processes** and **workflows**. Besides mentioning the fact that it is the type of transformation itself, we haven't discussed **Cloud** at all, which is the foundation for the agile business world that allows organizations to scale infrastructure as needed to support changing business priorities. We haven't talked yet about **test-driven development**, which is a major topic when it comes to test automation. All of these topics are essential and there are plenty of stories Vita could share, but we will continue to focus on people and people interactions. More precisely, in this section, we will focus on people interacting with bots, **Artificial Intelligence (AI) bots**. They may or may not solve one of the biggest stress factors for many humans on this earth, but anything to do with bots and robots is worth discussing in Vita's opinion!

A conversation with a former colleague happened only a few months ago, but this particular colleague Vita met very early in her leadership journey, which shows just how some relationships we build at work are so impactful, they withstand years, even if there is a gap in that time.

Vita first met Ankush in Bangalore when she went there on her very first business trip. Ankush was a program manager at the time and now was the owner and CEO of an AI company called CoRover. Ever since Vita took a course at MIT on business applications of AI and machine learning, she had been fascinated with the topic. She didn't consider herself an expert but, on a few occasions, when she was a part of strategic planning for digital transformation for a client, she would offer what she had learned over the last few years in the context of AI bots and how that technology could be leveraged. When she reconnected with Ankush after so many years and learned what his company did, she was extremely excited to interview Ankush to learn as much as possible on the topic.

Prior to asking Ankush for a somewhat formal interview, she learned that CoRover is the world's first human-centric conversational AI platform on a mission to clean up the customer service mess by enabling users to talk to any **ERP system** the way they talk to an intelligent person. CoRover was the first company to create an AI VideoBot, a software program for simulating human-like conversations using AI and machine learning.

Vita was familiar with the use of a chatbot within the customer support space, but she hadn't heard much about the concept of a video chat. When later in their conversation she asked Ankush to share a bit more details on what his company did he offered her the following:

"CoRover has the ability to engineer intelligent conversations between customers and organizations through the form of an omnichannel virtual assistant that can be interacted with through video, voice and text. CoRover creates the VideoBots using the audio, voice, and video of a real person to make the user believe that they are talking to a real person in real-time. These virtual assistants can be built to interact with users in 100+ foreign languages and 12+ Indian vernaculars. Also, the idea is instead of asking a user to come to our app, we will go where the user is, web, mobile app, SMS, Phone, Voice IVR, WhatsApp, WeChat, Line, Instagram, Twitter, Facebook, Kiosk, etc."

"That's incredible," Vita said. "I would love to play with it at some point. I would be curious to dive more into the technology itself at some point, but I would also love to ask you a few questions that are more general. I have had many interactions lately with product owners and leaders, discussing different types of value and what value means in different contexts. I would love to get your perspective on this since you are obviously thinking about bringing value to your clients and to your employees all the time. I am curious about your thoughts?"

Ankush responded: "Value is perceived differently by each individual and its definition has been argued about by generations of economists and philosophers.

John Ruskin, an English philosopher, took a more moral approach to the definition of value. I would actually like to read the full quote because I found it fascinating. He believed in the following, 'It is impossible to conclude, of any given mass of acquired wealth, merely by the fact of its existence, whether it signifies good or evil to the nation in the midst of which it exists. Its real value depends on the moral sign attached to it, just as strictly as that of a mathematical quantity depends on the algebraic sign attached to it. Any given accumulation of commercial wealth may be indicative, on the one hand of faithful industries, and on the other, it may be indicative of merciless tyranny.' Gandhi was greatly inspired by Ruskin's book and published a paraphrase of it in 1908.

The economic value is the amount an individual is willing to pay for a good or service while considering the money could be spent elsewhere. The economic value consists of its internal value (expense saving), external value (exchange value), and its opportunity cost (cost of opportunity foregone). Hence, for example, if the price of a good rises significantly due to inflation, this will lead to lower levels of demand for the product which will result in a fall in its economic value. In contrast, if there is an external consequence like the pandemic, the economic value of digital transformation services like virtual assistants will rise."

Vita needed time to process all of this information and said, "I think I would need to reread that quote a few times myself to fully follow it or see it visually to consume it better. Thank you for the follow up in your own words. It does make a lot of sense that there is internal value, external value and also cost of the opportunity foregone. We often talk about the cost of delay in decision making when we run leadership training, which is exactly that, the cost of opportunity foregone."

Ankush then concluded, "To survive, most companies will have to make revolutionary changes to key corporate processes. Simply treating digital transformation as a typical IT investment is insufficient and dangerous."

"Oh, could you elaborate on this, please?"

"Sure. The four horsemen of digital transformation are elastic cloud, big data, artificial intelligence, and the internet of things. The horsemen are rapidly spreading through every industry vertical, and it is no mere coincidence that they are spreading in tandem with the spread of coronavirus isolation and post-pandemic social and corporate policy."

"Ok, now I am actually going to ask you what research you have come across and used in your decision-making when it comes to your own company and the focus on AI bots. How did you decide that there was value in it?"

"Absolutely, we have used many resources but the one I can think of off the top of my head right now is Hubspot Research. It suggests that close to 70% of all business queries are either repeated verbatim or asked in a very similar template to that of previous questions. The customer service industry is a $350 billion industry and it is a complete mess: 33% of customers are most frustrated by having to wait on hold while 33% are most frustrated by having to repeat themselves to multiple support reps. (HubSpot Research). In a similar study, nearly 60% of customers feel that long holds and wait times are the most frustrating parts of a service experience. Many industry leaders believe that if we do not move customers from Email to a chat experience with built-in intelligent self-service then as an industry, we are doomed to escalating linear costs as more and more of humanity gets online with their smartphones and starts consuming digital services."

"I don't know about specific numbers, but I can tell you from personal experience, customer service is a huge mess and super annoying most of the time no matter who you are trying to reach. I am personally very excited about what your company offers. Can you talk a little bit about who uses your platform now and how CoRover maximizes value delivered to their clients?"

"CoRover's client are able to improve the top line sales figures by increasing the quality of customer interaction and thereby improve customer retention. The multilingual capability is also allowing companies to go global by eliminating the language barrier. They are also able to reduce the bottom-line expense figures from the cost savings of call centers. More importantly, they are also able to create an intangible effect by allowing these customer support agents who answer repeated queries all day to be involved with the company in a more creative capacity."

"This is so awesome. Who wouldn't want to do more creative work rather than answer repeated queries all day!? There is major value right there! Not only for the company's internal cost saving, but better service to customers and more interesting work for their employees! Alright, on this note, we will wrap this up and leave the audience wanting more! Thank you Ankush so much for your time. It was a pleasure!"

"Thank you, Vita!"

As Vita stopped the recording, she said, "I am so excited about your company and just your career journey in general. So much has happened since we met. Would you have believed if someone said a decade ago that you would start your own company and in the AI space too?"

"It is definitely surreal, no doubt," Ankush replied

7.7 Maximizing Value as a Change Agent

Over the years, Vita got the chance to be a full-time employee, often working with consultants, and then became a consultant herself working with many organizations. Throughout this process, she formed a pretty strong opinion on the fact that it should never be a US vs. THEM mentality. It is not about insiders vs. outsiders. The most value the organization can receive from change agents is if they have the right people in place.

Consultants bring a fresh perspective, observing without any bias, personal agendas or personal likes or dislikes. For consultants, it is not about the history or the fact that it has worked like this for over 30 years (as an example, Vita has heard as far back as 200 years at one client). Consultants see pain points and they focus on the right solution for the future. They can be more disruptive while challenging the "normal" ways of working, to make sure organizational inertia against the new change does not impact the transformation. At the same time, when you are an employee, you do understand the company and the challenges better, not to mention all the connections and relationships often needed to persuade folks to embrace something new.

Vita had come across the following quote which forced her to ponder on this for days.

> "Changing corporate culture is a humongous undertaking. Bringing an army of outside consultants that provide you with "best practices" is not the best way to earn the trust of people in your organization. Find the thought leaders inside your company and empower them to make decisions and drive change. Insiders

tend to understand the company business and have an ability to engage people around them."

Vita chuckled at first, appreciating the irony since she herself now was often part of the army of the outside consultants. Because Vita knew the person who wrote it, she thought about this person's experience and the reason behind this perspective, and it actually made a ton of sense.

From Vita's experience, there are a few reasons for a full-time employee to not appreciate consultants:

1. Their own opinion is not heard and/or their experience is not appreciated by the leadership. It could be reality or perception but if this is what employees think, these perceptions might as well be reality.

2. They perceive consultants as having absolutely no stake in the ground and no accountability for any outcomes. This is the case where consultants are hired only to help with strategy but have absolutely no connection to the implementation of that strategy.

3. They were forced to work with consultants without understanding what benefit they brought. Consultants came in, interviewed hundreds of people and nobody ever saw the results of that effort because leadership wasn't transparent in the findings, so to the people, it was a wasted effort.

In reality, based on Vita's experience, people are people and just like among full-time employees, there are consultants that are accountable, take pride in their work and truly care about the success of the organization, even if they do not plan to retire there. What makes the best team of change agents does not depend on whether you are a consultant or a full-time employee. It depends on putting together the team of people who are right for the job and see value in their personal accountability.

7.8 Maximizing Value of a Digital Transformation

One can describe a digital transformation in four dimensions, if not more.

1) *Business model transformation:* Focused on fundamental building blocks of how values are delivered in a specific industry such as Uber, Apple, Netflix

2) *Business process transformation:* Focused on reducing cycle time, lowering costs, improving quality through AI, machine learning, and analytics

3) *Domain transformation:* Focused on redefining products or services or creating a new type of value such as Amazon own streaming platform (Amazon Prime)

4) *Cultural/organizational transformation:* Redefining organizational capabilities, mindset, talent, and process

To achieve a true transformation and cover all these four dimensions is only possible through **Business Agility**. According to Dean Leffingwell, creator of Scaled Agile Framework Enterprise (SAFe): "Achieving a state of business agility means that the entire organization - not just development - is engaged in continually and proactively delivering innovative business solutions faster than the competition." This concept of optimizing whole suits also goes *very well with the **system thinking** concept presented by Russel Ackoff, 'A system is never the sum of its parts, it's the product of their interaction.' Hence to achieve the ultimate effectiveness of an organization, one has to optimize it as a whole and not as a part.*

Sevak Markarian
Executive Coach

A good example of optimizing the whole system, as opposed to just its parts, is developing policies, procedures, and incentives that are all interconnected. People are a major focus of an organizational change, and the outcome of a transformation will be much more successful when we achieve organizational alignment.

HR and finance need to be part of the whole system, just like other partners such as sales, marketing, infrastructure, facilities, etc., from the very start of a transformation. We need to look at the organization as a whole.

For example, the way projects are funded and people are assigned affects the organizational structure and accountability. If an employee is expected to do something different in an agile environment, but their job description or their performance review structure did not change, they may not be motivated to execute their new function. To them, it is just a nuisance and an addition to their full-time job. They may be perceived as not accountable which is detrimental to their career and the organization.

Bringing all parts of the organization in alignment and executing changes holistically prevents this situation.

With that said, if we find ourselves in the situation where the transformation has to start in a small pocket of the organization and others have to be persuaded to come along, we need to look at it as something we can experiment with and learn from. Of course, it can cause a few stressful moments here and there but it is all about how we look at it. Challenges like these, when not all the right people are at the table and neither business agility nor systems thinking are familiar terms to the leadership team who are leading the transformation, contribute to our learning and growth. It is the challenges that we face and learn from that make us the strongest change agents and transformation leaders we can be!

Whether it be the pivot to take advantage of a great new technology on the horizon or the resilience as an organization to handle a pandemic that will change how people interact and accomplish work, at its core, digital transformation will set the organization up for the opportunities and challenges of the future.

7.9 Exercise

Prepare for a Value Definition Workshop: Who are your customers? How do you maximize the value of your product, service, or role?

1. Define your internal and external customers. Whose day is affected by the existence of your product/service/role?

2. What problems do you solve for your customers? How would their day be different if your product/service/role did not exist?

3. What is a unique capability/service that only you can provide to your customers? Or what is your wow factor?

4. What other problems do your customers have that are related or adjacent to your product/service/role that you could be solving?

5. What feedback loops could you use to solicit your customers' input to validate your ideas, so you can maximize the value you deliver?

Illustration 7c. Maximizing Value Delivered

Conclusion

As promised during the introduction, no monsters or magic potions were discussed in this book and any reference to the Harry Potter series stopped after the attention of the reader was grabbed. However, we did use quite a few magic wands in the exercises we included at the end of each chapter.

One of the most potent magic tricks in digital transformation is the ability to FYAIL — or Face Yet Another Important Lesson. Reshaping an organization is a very complex endeavor wrought with multiple obstacles along the way. It's important to continuously reflect on these obstacles, learn our lessons, and adjust the course. The challenges that we face make us strong change agents and transformation leaders.

We have seen how limiting beliefs can stand in the way of our progress. Doubts stunt our growth and one of the most common misperceptions in digital transformation is that just because something has worked the same way for many years, it has to stay this way. It doesn't.

Recognizing limiting beliefs for what they are, just figments of our thinking and not the reality, unlocks the potential for both personal and organizational growth.

As a transformation unfolds, it is common to see misalignments in expectations, seeming lack of accountability, conflict, resistance, apathy, you name it. It is important to focus and uncover root causes of these issues, rather than trying to address the symptoms. The deeper concerns often lie in the organizational structure, incentives, and overall business agility.

We talked about how important it is to have a vision for our transformation, defining exactly what the change is and having an organizational alignment on the direction of the transformation. We discussed the fact that transformation is a journey and even when you accomplish your vision, a new vision will emerge. Change is always happening around us and how we build the resilience to handle it is part of the benefit of going through a healthy transformation.

Another key magic ingredient of a successful digital transformation is being objective about our progress in the chosen direction. We need to measure what really matters and that could vary from organization to organization and depends on the desired outcomes. Key metrics need to be discussed, collaborated, and aligned on! Exercise in section 5.9 along with a strong facilitator can help with that.

We shared a lot of personal stories along with our experiences and observations. We shared and poured our hearts out in order to encourage and reinforce that when we replace the fear of failing with the excitement of learning, we have an extremely high chance to succeed in digital transformations and so much more in life!

Conclusion

Illustration e. THE END

About Author

Luba Sakharuk started her professional journey as a software engineer with a Master's Degree in Computer Science from Worcester Polytech Institute of Technology. Her career led her to agile coaching, facilitation, leadership, consulting, and digital transformations.

While continuing her full-time employment as a senior lead consultant, she published two books and founded RALM3 Consulting LLC, focusing on public speaking and facilitation.

Luba lives in Framingham, Massachusetts with her husband and two beautiful and best behaving teenagers. She can often be found on the ski slopes of Loon Mountain in New Hampshire or taking long walks along Craigville Beach, on Cape Cod.

Q. How did you decide on who would be a contributing author?
A. It was less about who I would choose but more of a *what would inspire them to become a contributing author?* I have worked with all of these amazing women over the years and I knew there was so much expertise

and different perspectives, I wanted to collaborate and get their stories shared in addition to mine. I also wanted to share the journey of writing a book with them in case this is something that would be of interest to any of them in the future.

Q. Was this book written with a specific gender in mind?
A. Initially, given that I have been mentoring Women in Tech for a while and I do have two daughters, I wanted to share my professional journey in a male-dominated technology world. I also wanted to show off my female colleagues. The main message ended up being about the power of continuous learning and it is meant to inspire and educate all our youth about STEM.

About Contributing Authors

Alina Aronova

Alina Aronova is SVP of technology operations at Cengage. She is responsible for driving meaningful business transformation and operational maturity through the development and implementation of strategic and tactical initiatives across all functional areas of the technology group. She is also in charge of the management and execution of all activities for the chief technology officer's transformation office and oversees the program management organization, learning & development and agile teams. With a strong track record in business transformation in diverse functional areas, industries, and organizations from start-ups to global enterprises, Alina is committed to tackling the challenges and complications that companies face in a multitude of stages. She has an ability to build actionable and executional workflows to deliver results.

Prior to joining Cengage in 2014, Alina was VP of process management for SharkNinja where she drove new business development, built a center of excellence, and overhauled the talent strategy in the program management function. Prior to Euro-Pro, she spent three years at the John Hancock Life Insurance Company, where she was responsible for ensuring the completion of global regulatory and compliance initiatives, rolling out project management processes and infrastructure and directing global-scale IT projects. Alina has a reputation amongst her colleagues as a trusted advisor, natural relationship builder and persuasive change evangelist. She holds an MBA from Babson College and a bachelor's degree from Northeastern University. She resides in Newton, MA with her husband and two sons.

Q. Knowing what you know now, what advice would you give your younger self?
A. The advice I would give to my younger self: learn to trust your judgment earlier in your career. There is learning in every experience, good or bad. Another advice: There is no secret magic in good leadership, only hard work, common sense, logic, and empathy towards other people. Empathy might even be more critical than everything else. I am still learning that.

Q. What are some of the deciding factors for you when choosing a job?
A. When choosing a new job, I am assessing what I can learn from it that I do not know already. Would my manager push me further than I thought I was capable of? I also want to feel very intimidated and excited at the same time because it shows me that I will be stretching myself in a new role. I do not want to have a comfortable feeling when starting a new job.

Q. What is your philosophy when approaching challenging coaching situations?
A. When presented with a challenging coaching situation, I like to approach it from a place of curiosity rather than a problem-solving mindset and personal experience. At the end, clients always know what their best solution is but might need some support, discovering or uncovering it and validating it for themselves.

About Contributing Authors

Asmita Malse Dharap

LinkedIn: https://www.linkedin.com/in/asmita-dharap-pmp-1220bb29/

Asmita Malse Dharap is a highly motivated and impactful leader with a strong sense of purpose and passion for building quality products. She has extensive experience in a breadth of technologies and industries from start-up to mature companies. She is an agile enthusiast with focus on process excellence, continuous improvement, and change management. She excels in collaborating with cross functional teams, gaining alignment, and building strong, motivated teams. She is very team oriented and resonates with servant leadership principles. Asmita is continually on the look-out for ways to bring operational rigor to her team's work and proactively pursues identified opportunities.

After her Bachelor's Degree in Electronics and Telecommunications from India, she moved to the US to pursue her Master's Degree in Computer Science from IIT Chicago. She is a certified project management professional (PMP) and an established thought leader in quality space.

She currently lives in Michigan with her husband and two daughters and enjoys spending time outdoors.

Q. Knowing what you know now, what advice would you give your younger self?
A. Believe in yourself and take a moment to breathe and celebrate your achievements. Participate and engage rather than isolate.

Q. What are some of the deciding factors for you when choosing a job?
A. Other than the obvious ones, I want to make sure I can align with the leadership style and vision of my direct leader and the company

has a healthy, transparent, and positive culture that prioritizes its employees.

Q. What made you decide to contribute to this book?
A. This book is a dialogue very relevant in today's technological set up. I would like the readers to benefit and learn from these real-life examples and apply them to the situations they are navigating.

Jennifer Clarke-Burke

Jennifer Clarke-Burke Jennifer is an agilest who leads organizations through digital enterprise transformations. She has provided delivery-focused agile coaching in industries including financial services, insurance, pharmaceuticals, and retail. Jennifer is a passionate coach who works with individuals and teams at all levels of the organization and meets them where they are in the agile journey. She has experience as a coach, scrum master, program manager, and project manager. Outside of work, Jennifer enjoys spending time with her family and lake life in Maine.

Q. What would you advise your younger self?
A. Technology may be binary, but life is not. Believing there is no place for emotion in the workplace was incorrect. Embrace and expand your EQ!

Q. What was the most bizarre thing that ever happened to you in the corporate world?
A. Walking into a cubical where two men were reading a Playboy magazine and they didn't put it away. When I reported it to my manager, he made me feel like I was in the wrong for reporting it.

Q. How did you handle the situation after you reported the incident and felt as if you were in the wrong?
A. Because my manager minimized it and made me feel as though I was wrong, I didn't pursue any additional actions. I did change my behavior by 1) limiting contact with the individuals, 2) as I had gone directly from the incident to the manager's office, I processed situations before acting on them, 3) avoided emotion in the office. Looking back, I was working in a man's world and my manager probably didn't think there was anything wrong with what happened or if he did, he had no idea how to handle it!

Jennifer Greve

Jennifer Greve is a collaborative, dynamic professional with experience in digital transformations, agile product delivery, and organizational change management. She is a talented communicator and coach capable of building trust with individuals and groups at all levels of an organization, particularly those undergoing transformation. She brings an analytical yet human-centered approach to problem solving, process improvement, and guiding teams. Through her career she has moved between business and technology roles looking for increasingly complex situations to explore through various industries including finance and insurance, publishing, and educational technology. Her explorations led her to Consulting where she is passionate about applying her broad experience to helping teams and organizations solve a variety of challenges

Q. Do you have a favorite quote?
A. Celebrate your successes and failures; both require great courage!

Q. What would you advise your younger self?
A. Life really is a journey — you will have opportunities you couldn't imagine and face challenges that will feel insurmountable. Be patient with yourself, don't be afraid to ask for help, and remember to breathe.

Naomi Kent

Naomi Kent has over 15 years of experience in large and small organization transformations with a focus on agility in well-established environments. She has worked with various departments to help the culture and strategy align with the goals of the organization. She has seen success with motivating leaders and teams move forward to deliver on the promise of the change. She has worked in global and domestic financial and non-profit industries as a change agent. She is continuing her studies with a focus on culture, communication, and leadership to better help her clients address challenges. On a personal note, you may hear her cat in a remote video conference, and she enjoys chatting about her travels around the world.

Q. What is your philosophy when approaching challenging coaching situations?
A. A mantra I have said to myself since I was 10 years old still applies to my life now: Everything is a learning experience. The idea that every situation has something I can learn and it will end is important for me to continue with a coaching mindset. This is how I'm able to manage myself in challenging situations and then be better able to help other people and organizations.

Q. If you were to talk to anyone about a coaching career path, what is one thing you would emphasize?
A. I have found over the course of my coaching career that it incorporates all of my experience, skills, and identity. A lot of career paths only use part of your abilities and you lose the chance to exercise the other abilities over time. Coaching has allowed me to dust off skills I used in high school and university (event organizing) because it really has the potential to go in any direction. Some people would not like that greyness to the role, however for the folks that thrive in that space it can be a rewarding career.

Nadia Clifford

Nadia Clifford has over 20 years of hands-on experience delivering complex technology initiatives and has been at the forefront of digital business transformations across a diverse range of industry leaders in retail, media, financial services, and technology. She not only propels delivery forward through more efficient processes, but she does also it while encouraging positive collaboration and harnessing group intelligence. Nadia is especially adept at building empowered self-organizing teams, creating visibility into internal processes, fostering clear communication channels, and transforming silos into connected structures.

Most recently, Nadia completed MIT's digital transformation program and served as a change leader and a trusted business advisor for a cryptocurrency program at a large financial services firm.

Outside of work, Nadia is an avid endurance runner and loves to combine her trail runs with listening to audiobooks on all subjects – such as business, personal growth, spiritual, and fiction, including Russian contemporary literature.

Q. What are some of the deciding factors for you when choosing a job?
A. I always look for a challenge and an opportunity to grow. I have never taken a job that I had done previously. It's always been a leap of faith that I could step up to the challenge and out of my comfort zone. Another deciding factor is a cultural fit for me, I look for values very similar to mine.

Q. Do you have a favorite quote?
A. I have many! When I coach, I like to repeat bite-sized quotes until they become a part of the organization's vocabulary. Here are three of my favorites that I use all the time.

1. The best way to manage dependencies is to not have any.
2. Prioritization is not about saying YES to the critical work, it is about saying NO to everything else and focusing on just one thing at a time.
3. Prioritize ruthlessly

Q. What is your philosophy when approaching challenging coaching situations?
A. My philosophy is to listen, stay open, and trust my intuition. All those years of experience manifest themselves in our gut feelings. I like to define the outcome I want to achieve before I start a difficult conversation, but seek to understand first, check all my assumptions at the door and assume I know nothing about the situation. I ask questions and guide my coachees to their own conclusions. I do not tell people what to do, instead I try to understand what their goals are and help them figure out better ways of achieving those goals.

Natalie Vinitsky

https://www.linkedin.com/in/nvinitsky/

Natalie Vinitsky is an accomplished senior leader who specializes in helping organizations gain higher delivery value, sustain ongoing growth, and continuously improve by focusing on human centric design that includes both customers and employees.

Natalie is a dynamic change agent dedicated to helping organizations reinvent themselves by centering on aligning initiatives with corporate strategy and vision. Natalie possesses high-end practical experience building an agile practice to support organizational transformations at scale, creating agile driven operating models, and consultation services.

Natalie is an expert communicator, presenter, collaborator, and a frequently thought-out industry expert who can inspire change.

Q. Knowing what you know now, what advice would you give your younger self?
A. Be positive, driven, and persistent. Anything is possible if you want it. Observe, learn, reflect, and adjust always!

Q. What was the most bizarre thing that ever happened to you in the corporate world?
A. There were a few. One of them is when I was running a requirements document review in order to get a final signoff from stakeholders. A few people knocked on the conference room door and asked me and another 12 participants to vacate the room that they booked for a client visit. I booked the room as well and was so engaged in the review worrying about missing the deadline that I didn't want to cut it short. Given that

the room was double booked, I was there first and other rooms were available, I suggested they let me stay. Turns out I kicked out a big boss! Three lessons learned. For me, knowing your company leadership and customer comes first. For the boss, fix the outlook double-booking issue, which he did in two weeks.

Tatiana Thomas

Tatiana Thomas is leading digital transformation at Analog Devices. She combines technology, creativity, leadership, and integrity to help teams and companies reach their potential. She began her career as an immigrant with a Russian education in mathematical modeling of optical systems. She restarted from the ground floor in the United States as a user interface programmer with a keen appreciation for the display of beautiful data.

Tatiana rapidly moved into information architecture and product design while also exploring her love for teaching and combined these passions to create a dynamic style of managing teams. This brought her into contact with marketing, and she quickly learned to create value at the nexus between product development, user experience, and marketing. She launched her own consulting business dedicated to supporting startups by helping them optimize their product design and user experience strategies, which gave her an opportunity to apply hands-on skills with visibility at the most senior levels in the organization.

In 2014, Tatiana joined a technology incubator at Altisource Labs to help spin out new technologies and lead teams that defined entirely new-to-the-world products from a design thinking approach. A year ago, Tatiana joined Analog Devices to lead the digital transformation initiative across the organization, accelerating their growth by reimagining their product and technical marketing from a client-centric perspective.

Q. Knowing what you know now, what advice would you give your younger self?
A. My work advice to myself is actually nearly the same as the one I would give myself in non-work situations. Listen to your inner voice, don't care too much about what other people think.

Q. What are some of the deciding factors for you when choosing a job?
A. I'm always looking for a challenge, not to others, but for myself. Position that allows me to use my brains and my skills to build something worth building. Something that will have an impact on other people's lives and make their work or life easier and more meaningful. It is also important that the job you are being hired for is recognized as important inside of the organization and is supported by corporate leadership.

Q. What is your philosophy when approaching challenging coaching situations?
A. Coaching is almost never easy, but I spend a considerable amount of my working time coaching and educating. I believe that the most important element of coaching is to find what is important to a specific person or a group of people and try to connect to that. Approach coaching as an opportunity to help someone in their work. If people understand that you are not trying to impose your agenda on them, but trying to help them, they are much more receptive to your suggestions. Good sense of humor and the ability to stay positive in any situation is also necessary.

Acknowledgements

First and foremost, I would like to thank my amazing colleagues, the contributing authors, without whom this book just simply would not be possible. Their passion for the topic, their expertise, their wisdom, and willingness to prioritize this effort is greatly appreciated! **Alina Aronova, Asmita Malse Dharap, Jennifer Clarke-Burke, Jennifer Greve, Naomi Kent, Nadia Clifford, Natalie Vinitsky, and Tatiana Thomas:** THANK YOU!

I would like to thank **Victoria Yampolsky, Ankush Sabharwal,** and **Sevak Markarian** for sharing their wisdom, experience, and expertise and allowing me to interview them, as well as include their stories and their quotes in this book. Their contribution is very much appreciated!

I would like to thank my husband and children for staying out of my basement office and often fetching their own dinners because when one is in the writing mode, they better not be disturbed!

I would like to thank all of my LinkedIn and Facebook friends and supporters who encouraged me throughout the process, provided honest feedback, and showed enough enthusiasm for this effort to fuel the energy it takes to keep going, ignore cold feet and publish the book regardless of any second thoughts or insecurities which randomly pop up in one's head when one shares their writing.

I would like to thank the Ultimate 48h Author Publishing team, designers, illustrators, editors, proofreaders, and everyone who contributed to this book in any way, shape, or form! It takes a village, and I am grateful for mine!

Call to Action

1. Connect with Luba Saharuk on LinkedIn via the following QR Code,

Luba Sakharuk
Sr. Lead Consultant at Apex Systems | Author | Speaker

2. Visit www.ralm3.com or use the following QR Code to book a speaking engagement!

3. Find RALM3 Facebook group using the following QR Code!

Glossary

Note: Definitions here came either straight from Wikipedia, Google search or were defined by the author or the contributing authors as they saw the most accurate based on their experience. These are meant to be quick refreshers/learnings as you are reading the book, so that you don't have to put the book away to look them up.

DO NOT MAKE ANY LIFE DECISIONS BASED ON THESE DEFINITIONS!!!

A

Agile - Agile is a methodology. It is a way of working. It started out in the world of software development but the concept of breaking up large chunks of work into smaller pieces to iterate and get feedback on, as well as transparency and collaboration is applicable and often used outside of software development.

Agile coach - Agile coaches come in different flavors with different backgrounds. At a minimum, they are experts in all agile related areas, from the mindset to the mechanics behind different frameworks that help achieve alignment, iterative approach, and transparency on all levels of the organization. Coaching is a separate skill in itself. Agile coaches may operate on a team level, program, or portfolio level, as well as Enterprise level. Some agile coaches may be excellent facilitators and trainers, and some may have deep expertise in Infrastructure and DevOps.

Agile Transformation - When an organization begins to use agile methodologies to develop software or build their products they may go through a transformation. Becoming agile involves shifting how we think about work, not just implementing new tools and processes.

Artificial Intelligence (AI) - Artificial intelligence (AI) is the ability of a computer or a robot controlled by a computer to do tasks that are usually done by humans because they require human intelligence

Automation - Automation describes a wide range of technologies that reduce human intervention in processes

Application Programming Interface (API) - Application Programming Interface is an intermediary that allows communication between software systems.

Architecture - Software architecture may be thought of as an organization of a system. This organization includes all components, how they interact with each other and the environment in which they operate.

B

Backlog - A prioritized list of the work items

Baseline - A starting measurement which will be used for comparison as you continue to make progress towards your goals.

Behavior Driven Development (BDD) - Behavior Driven Development is a software development approach that allows the tester/business analyst to create test cases in simple text language (English). The simple language used in the scenarios helps even non-technical team members to understand what is going on in the software project

Business Requirement Document (BRD) - The BRD describes the problems the project is trying to solve and the required outcomes necessary to deliver value.

Being Agile- Agility is a state of mind more than a set of practices. Organizations and individuals who are agile are more responsive to changing needs with less disruption to their workflow.

Being an Ass - To be an ass in the work environment means different things to different people. It really depends. If you yell at someone, you are being an ass. If you put someone down, you are being an ass. If you are demanding and expect high quality results, you may actually not be an ass. However, you may still be perceived as one. If you self-reflect and wonder if you had been an ass, you may still be an ass but there is hope for you!

Bot - A chatbot or chatterbot is a software application used to conduct an on-line chat conversation via text or text-to-speech, in lieu of providing direct contact with a live human agent

Business Owner - The business owner plays a strategic role and is not engaged in the day-to-day activities. They focus on the big picture. They define the vision and roadmap.

C

Chief executive officer (CEO) - The chief executive officer is generally the highest-ranking person in a company and they hold the ultimate accountability for the business.

Chief information officer (CIO) - The chief information officer is responsible for the organization's information and technology areas with a greater focus on internal operations and technology infrastructure.

Chief technology officer (CTO)- The chief technology officer is generally responsible for defining the strategy and vision for technology to meet customer's needs including overseeing software engineering and innovation.

Chief product officer (CPO) - The chief product officer is responsible for the company's product strategy and vision and oversees the people who design, develop, and manage those products.

Change Management - Change management involves approaching large-scale initiatives in a planned way that accounts for the impact to people, not just process. This can include things like assessing the organization's readiness for change, helping build plans to engage people in the process, and ensuring people have what they need to lead to a successful adoption.

C-Suite - This group is comprised of the highest-level executives in a company, e.g., CEO, CIO.

Change Agents - Someone who is a catalyst for change. They promote and enable changes in the organization.

Culture - An organization's culture drives how people behave. This can include formal components like vision and values, but it also includes the unwritten, often unspoken, "how we do business." Large organizations typically have different cultures across different departments. It can be important to take this into consideration when planning enterprise level transformations or change initiatives that span groups.

Coach - A coach is someone who provides guidance to another in a way that allows that individual or group to learn and grow and become independent.

Glossary

Center of Excellence (CoE) - A center of excellence is a team of skilled knowledge workers whose mission is to provide the organization they work for with best practices around a particular area of interest

D

DevOps - DevOps brings together practices from software development and IT operations that allow companies to release high quality code more quickly. This is accomplished through greater collaboration and automation through the software development lifecycle.

DevSecOps - DevSecOps extends DevOps practices to bring security integration into every step of the software development lifecycle.

Digital - All electronic instruments, automated systems, technical equipment, and resources that produce, process or store information are included in the definition of digital technology

Digital Solution - Digital solutions are very effective in improving business productivity as they eliminate various factors that affect business productivity. Digital solutions automate some tasks that would usually require humans, and thus eliminates human errors, resulting in a smoother, more resilient business operation.

Digital transformation- Digital transformation is the integration of digital technology into all areas of a business, changing how you operate and deliver value to customers. It's also a cultural change that requires organizations to continually challenge the status quo, experiment, and get comfortable with failure (or in the context of this book, **FACING YET ANOTHER IMPORTANT LESSON (FYAIL)**)

E

Enterprise - Enterprise as a project or for-profit business or company. It is most often associated with entrepreneurial ventures. According to some definitions, enterprises are generally considered large corporations that manage hundreds or even thousands of employees.

Executive - A business executive is a person responsible for running an organization, although the exact nature of the role varies depending on the organization. Executives run companies or government agencies. They create plans to help their organizations grow

Enterprise Coach - The enterprise coach has a holistic view of an organization and works across boundaries to accelerate the business agility journey. The enterprise coach is uniquely positioned to partner with organizational leadership to co-create meaningful and sustained change.

Enterprise Level - In the context of this book, when we say enterprise level, we mean the overall organization.

Executive Coach - An executive coach is a qualified professional that works with individuals (usually executives, but often high-potential employees) to help them gain self-awareness, clarify goals, achieve their development objectives, unlock their potential, and act as a sounding board

Extreme Programming - Extreme programming is a software development methodology which is intended to improve software quality and responsiveness to changing customer requirements

Epic - An agile epic is a body of work that can be broken down into specific tasks (called user stories) based on the needs/requests of customers or end-users.

Epic Cycle Time - The amount of time elapsed from when work starts on an epic to when it completes and can be delivered.

Glossary

Entrepreneur - A person who organizes and operates a business or businesses, taking on greater than normal financial risks in order to do so.

Estimation - A technique used to define how much effort it will take to complete a piece of work. Agile teams predominantly use relative sizing using a Fibonacci scale or T-shirt sizes.

Emotional Intelligence (EQ) - Emotional intelligence is most often defined as the ability to perceive, use, understand, manage, and handle emotions

F

Feedback - A feedback culture is a culture where every employee feels that they can share feedback with another person in the organization - regardless of role.

Framework - A framework is a particular set of rules, ideas, or beliefs which you use in order to deal with problems or to decide what to do.

Feature - A feature is a unit of functionality of a software system that satisfies a requirement, represents a design decision, and provides a potential solution

G

Growth Mindset - A belief that an individual always has the capacity to learn and that knowledge and ability is not fixed.

H

Human Resources (HR) - Human resources is used to describe both the people who work for a company or organization and the department responsible for managing all matters related to employees.

I

Information Overload - That is what this book can give someone for whom the topic of digital transformation is completely new! Sorry about that! We inserted fun illustrations to make up for it!

J

Jira - a software product for the management of work and workflows. This product is owned by Atlassian Software company.

Jira Align Plugin - Software components that can be integrated / installed with Jira that provide additional features/functions and reports on the Jira data.

K

Kanban - Where scrum is a framework specific to implementation of agile. Kanban is a framework specific to implementation of lean. Kanban only prescribes a handful of practices.

KPIs - A performance indicator or key performance indicator is a type of performance measurement. KPIs evaluate the success of an organization or of a particular activity in which it engages.

L

Legacy Systems - A legacy system is an old or outdated system, technology or software application that continues to be used by an organization because it still performs the functions it was initially intended to do.

Glossary

Lean - Lean thinking is a transformational framework that aims to provide a new way to think about how to organize human activities to deliver more benefits to society and value to individuals while eliminating waste

M

Microservices - A microservice architecture – a variant of the service-oriented architecture structural style – arranges an application as a collection of loosely-coupled services. In a microservices architecture, services are fine-grained, and the protocols are lightweight.

Methodology - In the context of this book, agile methodologies are approaches to product development that are aligned with the values and principles described in the Agile Manifesto for software development. Agile methodologies aim to deliver the right product, with incremental and frequent delivery of small chunks of functionality, through small cross-functional self-organizing teams, enabling frequent customer feedback and course correction as needed.

Middleware - Type of software that provides services from one application to another, often used in data integration or extraction between systems.

Mission - A mission statement is a short statement of why an organization exists, what its overall goal is, identifying the goal of its operations: what kind of product or service it provides, its primary customers or market, and its geographical region of operation.

Minimum viable product (MVP) - Minimum viable product is a new version of a product with just enough features to provide some value to a customer and to collect enough feedback that allows it to iterate and expand on the product.

N

North Star - The north star clearly outlines the entire company's transformation goals, allowing each function and business unit to begin to cascade those goals and tailor its charter accordingly.

Net Promoter Score - Net promoter score is a widely used market research metric that typically takes the form of a single survey question asking respondents to rate the likelihood that they would recommend a company, product, or a service to a friend or colleague.

O

Objectives and key results (OKRs) - Objectives and key results is a goal setting framework used by individuals, teams, and organizations to define measurable goals and track their outcomes. The development of OKR is generally attributed to Andrew Grove who introduced the approach to Intel during his tenure there.

Outcomes - Outcomes are the changes you expect to result from your program. These can be changes in individuals, systems, policies or whatever it is you are looking to achieve. They may reflect shifts in relationships, knowledge, awareness, capabilities, attitudes, and/or behaviors.

Outputs - The output is an action that you take towards your goals. Output are not measurable outcomes! Outcomes are the measurable results that you hope to see after you have finished your outputs. Outcomes are not about doing, they are about delivering real, valuable business results.

Glossary

P

Product owner - The primary goal of an agile product owner is to represent the customer to the development team. Product owner responsibilities include managing and prioritizing a product backlog.

Product Backlog - Product backlog refers to a prioritized list of functionalities which a product should contain. It is sometimes referred to as a to-do list.

Product Manager - A product manager is a professional role that is responsible for the development of products for an organization

Product Vision - A Product vision is a description of the essence of your product: what are the problems it is solving, for whom, and why now is the right time to build it.

Personas - Personas are fictional characters, which you create based upon your research in order to represent different folks who might use your service, product, solution or a platform. Creating personas helps you understand your users' experiences, behaviors, needs and goals.

PI Planning - PI Planning is a meeting of multiple teams working together where they meet to plan the roadmap, deliberate on features, and identify cross-team dependencies.

Production - In terms of technology, it is the environment where the product and code reside that is used by the consumers. Ex. When you stream from Netflix, you are using their production environment.

Psychologically safe - Psychological safety is being able to show and employ oneself without fear of negative consequences of self-image, status or career.

Q

Quality assurance (QA) - Quality assurance is a way of preventing mistakes and defects in products and avoiding problems when delivering products or services to customers

QA Automation - The ability to test the quality of a product or product change through software vs. manual quality tests.

R

Reviews (aka 360) - 360 review is a process of getting feedback on an individual's performance and/or potential from their manager and others who interact with them regularly, ie., peers, direct reports, manager's manager, etc.

Relative Sizing - Measuring the effort and complexity of work by comparing them to each other (relative to one another). Example - The work to deliver one piece of work is twice the size as another. Types of relative measurements are T-shirt sized (small, medium, large) and story pointing.

S

Scrum - Scrum is a lightweight framework that helps people, teams and organizations generate value through adaptive solutions for complex problems

Scrumban - A framework that incorporates some of the features of both the scrum and kanban frameworks. The features incorporated are determined by the organization, there is no industry standard definition. It uses agile principles and values to deliver business value.

Glossary

Scrum master - An individual who is responsible for the scrum process. The scrum master works with teams to guide them in the usage of the scrum framework.

Servant Leadership - A style of leadership where the leader 'serves' the people they lead. The leader's focus is to help individuals and teams become their best selves through ensuring that their needs are satisfied.

Spaghetti code - Spaghetti code is a pejorative phrase for unstructured and difficult-to-maintain source code. Spaghetti code can be caused by several factors, such as volatile project requirements, lack of programming style rules, and software engineers with insufficient ability or experience

Standard operating procedure (SOP) - A document describing steps to be performed in a specific business scenario.

Sprint - A time-boxed period where a team works to complete a specified amount of work.

Sprint Backlog - The specific work a team has identified for completion in a sprint.

Story Points - A relative measuring system used to estimate the effort and complexity of work. Most commonly, story points use a Fibonacci scale.

Scaled Agile Framework (SAFe) - They have a very detailed website with a diagram that allows you to click into different sections and dive deep.

Strategic financial modeling - A financial model allows a company to simulate their revenue and expenses under various situations.

ServiceNow - ServiceNow is a software company that develops a cloud computing platform to help companies manage digital workflows for enterprise operations

Service-level agreements (SLAs) - A contract between the consumer/user and supplier which states the level of service they can expect under certain conditions. Ex. You expect on-line access to your banking account 24X7 (24 hours a day, 7 days a week).

Scaling Framework - The scaled agile framework is a set of organization and workflow patterns intended to guide enterprises in scaling agile practices

Service-oriented architecture (SOA) - Service-oriented architecture, defines a way to make software components reusable and interoperable via service interfaces. Services use common interface standards and an architectural pattern so they can be rapidly incorporated into new applications.

T

Team - A group of individuals who work together for a common goal.

Test-driven development (TDD) - Test-driven development is a style of programming where coding, testing, and design are tightly interwoven.

Transformation - Transformation in tech industry is usually about technology, data, process, and organizational change

Technical Debt - In software development, technical debt is the implied cost of additional rework caused by choosing an easy solution now instead of using a better approach that would take longer.

U

UX - User experience design is the process design teams use to create products that provide meaningful and relevant experiences to users.

Glossary

UI – User interface is the series of screens, pages, and visual elements—like buttons and icons—that enable a person to interact with a product or service

User Story - Short, simple description from a user's perspective of something they desire or want, for example - a new feature in a product or a change in the product.

V

Vision - A vision statement is an inspirational statement of an idealistic emotional future of a company or group.

Velocity - The measurement of amount of work completed in a sprint (short timeframe). Common ways of measuring velocity is #story points, hours, or #stories completed.

Value – The importance, worth or usefulness of something. Chapter 7 dives deep into the topic of Value.

X

XP Extreme Programming. One of the agile frameworks.

"Listening is a major part of Public Speaking!" ~ Luba Sakharuk

RALM3

Able to adapt her presentations between 30 minutes to a full day program, Luba's three main keynotes are:

The Art of Persuasion

- How learning to ski made me a better Transformation Coach
- How knowing the Social Style of your peers makes you a more effective change agent
- How defining and communicating the change leads to alignment and a successful transformation

Luba Sakharuk

started her professional journey as a software engineer with a master's degree in Computer Science from Worcester Polytech Institute of Technology. Her career led her to Agile Coaching, Facilitation, Leadership, Consulting and Digital Transformations.

While continuing her full-time employment as a Sr. Lead Consultant, she published two books and founded RALM3 Consulting LLC, focusing on Public Speaking and Facilitation.

Luba lives in Framingham, Massachusetts with her husband and two beautiful and best behaving teenagers. She can often be found on the ski slopes of Loon Mountain in New Hampshire or taking long walks along Craigville Beach, on Cape Cod.

A highly engaging and inspiring presenter, Luba has spoken on her career journey and various other topics at industry events such as She+Geeks out, Women in Technology, as well the Women in Agile global conference. She has also appeared in various podcasts and facilitated hundreds of workshops, focusing on inspiring attendees to self-reflect on their own journeys and guide them towards that next step.

The Art of Maximizing Value Delivered

- How to recognize when your doubts are Limiting Beliefs
- How to find your core genius and maximize your personal value
- How to Maximize Value in Digital Transformations

The Art of Conflict Resolution

- How defining what success looks like leads to healthy change
- How choosing what to measure leads to data driven decisions
- How focusing on Continuous Learning reduces stress and leads to a Life Worth Living!

To engage **Luba** to speak at your next event, email **luba@lubasakharuk.com** for pricing and availability.

www.ingramcontent.com/pod-product-compliance
Lightning Source LLC
Chambersburg PA
CBHW021429080526
44588CB00009B/468